WILD RACES
OF
SOUTH-EASTERN INDIA.

WILD RACES
OF
SOUTH-EASTERN INDIA.

CAPT. T. H. LEWIN

GYAN

Published by

Gyan Publishing House
5, Ansari Road
Daryaganj, New Delhi-110002
Phone: 011-47034999, 9811692060
E-mail: books@gyanbooks.com

Distribution Network
gyanbooks.com
India, USA, Canada, UK, Australia, France

ISBN: 978-81-212-8372-4 (PB)
First Published, 1870

2nd Impression 2023

Printed at: Gyan Press, Delhi.

WILD RACES OF SOUTH-EASTERN INDIA
Author: T. H. LEWIN

WILD RACES

OF

SOUTH-EASTERN INDIA.

WILD RACES

OF

SOUTH-EASTERN INDIA.

BY CAPT. T. H. LEWIN,

Deputy Commissioner of Hill Tracts.

"I think that all details become interesting when they relate to, and serve to depict, the characteristics of people of whom we have known little until now, and with whom it is desirable to cultivate more intimate terms."—*Letter from Lieutenant Samuel Turner, Ambassador to Thibet, addressed to Mr. John Macpherson, Governor-General of Bengal, 2nd March,* 1784.

London:

WM. H. ALLEN & CO.,

13, WATERLOO PLACE.

1870.

Inscribed by Permission

TO

MRS. GEO. GROTE.

CONTENTS.

PART I.

THE HILL TRACTS.

PART II.

THE HILL TRIBES (SONS OF THE RIVER).

PART III.

THE HILL TRIBES (SONS OF THE RIVER)
Continued.

INTRODUCTION.

NOVELTY is as attractive now as ever it was, even in the days when the Athenians went about hearing or telling of some new thing. I think, therefore, that no apology is needed in introducing to English readers races of people of whom but little is known, and whose habits and customs have never before been described.

The mighty empire of Hindostan is now bound up by a hundred ties of interest with the present and future of England. Many are the hearths by which is kept sacred the empty place of some dear member of the family circle, who is absent in those torrid climes; and books relating any thing new of this far-off but no longer strange land of the East, are studied by all classes of English people with sentiments of growing attention and admiration for the great but unfinished work we are carrying on there.

These pages were written day by day among the people of whom they treat, during a three years' sojourn among them. Sometimes under the shelter of a straw-thatched bungalow on a remote hill top, with the pathless jungle undulating in vast sweeps of hill and dale beneath the gaze; at other times in boats, poling along the hill streams, or by the firesides of the people in their bamboo-houses, perched securely in some hillside nook. The work was commenced at first with no fixed plan as to a detailed account of these races of men; indeed, as one of their many proverbs says, "Unlaid eggs cannot be counted;" but I simply noted down as I heard them any tales, traditions, or striking customs that fell under my observation in the course of my wanderings among them. Little by little, however, my interest was awakened and my affections drawn to them: I found them a people worthy of esteem, worthy of note. It is unfortunately too often the custom among English people, as a body, to contemn and despise all races speaking an alien tongue; among the commonalty at the present time even, the French are regarded as an outlandish and ignorant people; while as for people like these hill races, whose skin is dark and breech bare, out and alack! they are savages and barbarians forsooth, very little better, indeed, than the apes among whom they reside. I have, nevertheless, found among all wild and so-called barbarous races, that when one grows acquainted with their language, and they, becoming habituated to you, allow a knowledge of their social life and habits, they are very much the same as other people; there is not much difference, indeed, between human nature all the world over,—they love and hate, eat and drink, live and die, in much the same, and often in a far more natural and sensible manner than we of the civilized races, who hold ourselves so loftily aloof in our fancied intellectual and moral superiority. It would seem almost a solecism to announce this fact as if it were some novel discovery; but any one who has lived in the East and seen our Englishmen, whether Government officials, merchants, or planters, will, with some rare exceptions, find that they know, and care to know, nothing of the people they are thrown among—they are with them but not of them—hardly troubling themselves, indeed, to become acquainted with the language of the people among whom they live, and never admitting them, or seeking themselves any admission into social intimacy or friendship. Broad and umbrageous as is the tree of our Eastern Government at present, this is the canker that will eventually eat it through at the root, until it fall with a crash, in ruin.

This very book is a proof of my assertion. We have been living at the door of these hill races, and in close contact with them for more than eighty years, and yet no Englishmen (Government officials or otherwise) that I ever met, knew any thing of them in any way, save that perhaps they were dully conscious of the proximity of certain hill tribes, who, as was stated in an official document quoted in the body of this work, "go unclothed, and know not the use of fire-arms."

It is, then, into the private life of these

simple and primitive races that I venture to introduce my readers; to make them, if so it may be, partakers of wild hospitality, and intimate with the domestic society of men and women—children of Nature.

WILD RACES OF SOUTH-EASTERN INDIA.

PART I.

THE HILL TRACTS.

RISING from the rice swamps and level land of the Chittagong District, of which it forms the eastern boundary, there stretches out a vast extent of hilly and mountainous country, inhabited by various hill races. Of this country and of these people I purpose here to give some account, but more especially I shall notice such part of it as, lying between Lat. 21° 25′ and 23° 45′ north, and

Long. 91° 45′ and 92° 50′ east, is subject to British rule, and distinguished by the name of the Chittagong Hill Tracts.

The country in question lies on the south-eastern shores of the Bay of Bengal, and is bounded on the west by the maritime District of Chittagong; on the south and east, as far as the Blue Mountain, by the Province of Arracan; on the north, by the Fenny River, which divides the Hill Tracts from Hill Tipperah, a semi-independent State; while to the north and north-east the boundary is undefined, and may be said to be conterminous with the extent to which the influence of the British Government is acknowledged amongst the hill tribes in that direction.

The extent of the district, however, may be roughly summarized as the country watered by the Rivers Fenny, Kurnafoolee, Sungoo, and Matamooree, with their tributaries from the water-sheds to the entry of these rivers into the Chittagong District.

The River Fenny and the western major tributaries of the Kurnafoolee have their sources in the range of hills from which, on the other side, rises the Dallesur and Gotoor streams, which again are affluent of the River Barak in Cachar.

The Kurnafoolee[1], or, to call it by its hill name, the Kynsa Khyoung, has its rise in a lofty range of hills to the north-east; from this same range springs the Sonai and Tipai streams, tributaries of the Barak in Cachar, and the Koladan or Koladyne River, which last debouches into the Indian Ocean at Akyab in Arracan.

The Sungoo[2], or Rigray Khyoung, and the Matamooree, or Moree Khyoung, take their rise in the range of hills which divides Arracan from the Chittagong Hill Tracts on the south-east. Of these two rivers, the Kurnafoolee is the principal. It is navigable at all seasons of the year, for boats of considerable

[1] Kurnah, an ear (Sanscrit); foolee, or phoolie, from phool, flower. The Mahommedan Wuzeer during the Moghul rule is said to have dropped his earring into the river; hence the name.

[2] Sungoo, from sunkh, a shell.

size, as far as 20 miles beyond Kassalong, one of our frontier guard-posts; but here all further progress is stopped by the Burkhul rapids, which offer an insurmountable obstacle to further progress. Above Burkhul the river narrows considerably, as it enters the higher ranges of hills: its course has not been followed further than the Demagree falls, some three days' journey above Burkhul. Boats, however, can proceed three days' journey northwards up the Kassalong and Chingree streams, both of which are tributaries of the Kurnafoolee. The scenery along the course of the Kurnafoolee and its tributaries is for the most part dull and uninteresting, the river flowing between high banks of earth, covered either with tall elephant grass or dense jungle, which effectually prevent any view being obtained of the surrounding country. At one place only on the Kurnafoolee, shortly after reaching the small Police Station of Rangamuttee, the character of the scenery changes from its usual dull monotony of reaches of still water and walls of dark green verdure to a scene of marvellous beauty, resembling somewhat the view on the Rhine, near the Lurleiberg. Dark cliffs of a brown vitreous rock, patched and mottled with lichens and mosses of various colours, tower up on either hand; while occasionally, on the right or left, shoots back a dark gorge of impenetrable jungle. At this place the river runs with great rapidity through a rocky defile, and at some seasons of the year it is difficult for boats to make head against the strength of the current.

The character of the scenery on the Fenny River is much the same as that of the Kurnafoolee. Here and there on the banks of the stream, or perched on the ridge of some adjacent hill, may be seen the houses of the hill men; and they and their families, the women in quaint distinctive dress, grouped themselves on the bank, to observe our boats going up. The sources of the Fenny River have not been visited or surveyed.

The rivers in the southern part of the

district differ considerably from those of the north. The country is more rocky, and the adjacent hill ranges narrower and of greater height. The River Sungoo is known by three names. In the upper portion of its course it is called Rigray Khyoung by the hill men; about midway, before entering the plains, it is known as the Sabuk Khyoung; while in the plains, the Bengallees have given it the name of the Sungoo. It is a clear stream, running for the most part of its hill course over sand and among rocks; it abounds in small rapids, and in its higher parts is navigable only to the smallest boats. Ordinary-sized boats of burden can, in the dry season, go no further than a place called Bundrabun.

The Matamoree, or Moree Khyoung, is a shallow and not very important stream, running parallel for a great part of its course with the Sungoo, although the rivers debouch by different mouths into the sea. Although the course of the river itself is monotonous, yet up some of its affluents, particularly as they near their sources in the hills, the scene becomes one of unmixed beauty. I remember once going up the Twine Khyoung, a tributary of this river. The stream ran briskly in a narrow pebbly bed, between banks that rose nearly perpendicularly, and so high that the sun only came down to us by glints, here and there. Enormous tree ferns hung over our heads, some 50 feet up, while the straight stems of the "Gurjun" tree shot up without a branch, like white pillars in a temple; plantains, with their broad drooping fronds of transparent emerald, broke at intervals the dark-green wall of jungle that towered up in the background, and from some gnarled old forest giant here and there the long curving creepers threw across the stream a bridge of nature's own making. Sometimes we came upon a recess in the bank of verdure which rose on either hand; and there the tinkling of a cascade would be heard behind the veil, its entry into the stream being marked by a great gray heap of rounded rocks and boulders, toppled and tossed about in a way that showed with what a sweep the water came down in the rains. Scarlet dragonflies and butterflies of purple, gold, and azure, flitted like jewels across our path; while silvery fish, streaked with dark-blue bands, flew up the stream before us, like flashes of light, as we poled along.

The western limit of China, the Province of Yunan, is shown in the map as about 97° 98′ degrees of Longitude east, in the Parallel of 24°. Our eastern frontier, then, is not more than 300 miles from the western boundary of China. The tribes in that direction are known to have intercourse with the Province of Meckley, subject to the King of Burmah, and it seems not improbable that at some future time a practicable route might be discovered between the sea-port of Chittagong and the eastern portion of the Empire of China.

This idea was contemplated as early as 1761, when Mr. Harry Verelst, the Chief of Chittagong, wrote to the President of the Council, Fort William, that "we have reason to believe that a passage may be found through the mountains of Tconke [3] into Thibet and the northern parts of Cochin China. Although this may be a work of time, yet, when effected, it may redound greatly to the State of Europe."

The area of the Chittagong Hill Tracts is estimated to be 6796 miles. The most noticeable feature of the country is that it is divided into four river valleys, marked out more or less distinctly by well-defined chains of hills running parallel from the south in a north-westerly direction. The Sungoo and Matamoree Rivers, until they enter the plains, run parallel to the hill ranges, forming two of the river valleys alluded to. The Kurnafoolee and Fenny Rivers, however, run transversely across the line of the hills. The river valleys here are formed by large tributary streams entering the Kurnafoolee at right angles to its course.

[3] No such place as Tconke is known to us now; but as Mr. Verelst was reporting on the prospects and resources of the Chittagong District, it seems not unlikely that he referred to the hills which abut thereon.

The soil of the district is composed for the most part of a rich loam, but in many parts the hills are found to consist of a schistose clay, much resembling sand-stone in appearance, which falls to pieces very easily on force being applied. In the alluvial valleys and watercourses large pieces of dicoly-tedonous wood are frequently found lying in a horizontal position: they are usually more or less petrified.

The climate of the Hill Tracts is distinguished by two characteristics; its coolness, and its unhealthiness as regards foreigners. There are no hot winds in the hills, and the hottest part of the year is tempered by cool sea-breezes. It is the custom of the people to remain in their villages until the cultivation season commences in May, and then the whole country-side moves up, every man to his patch of cultivation, on some lofty hill. It is to this custom, I consider, that their comparative immunity from sickness may be traced, for hill men, on abandoning their usual mode of life, and taking to other occupations not involving the periodical move to the hill tops, are nearly as much subject to fever as the people of the plains.

During the months of November, December, January, and February, dense fogs settle over the hills during the night, seldom clearing away until the middle of the following day. Those fogs, however, do not seem to have an unhealthy effect, as the four months in which they prevail are the healthiest throughout the year. During the month of February some rain generally falls, but the rainy season does not set in until the end of May or beginning of June, when it continues, almost without intermission, until the end of September. The quantity of rain that falls is very large, the average yearly fall being about 120 inches. During the rainy season, it is well-nigh impossible to move about the country on account of the rising of the hill streams. Before the setting in of the rains, the hill people lay in a stock of provisions, as at that season of the year the bazaars are abandoned by the men of the plains, and trade almost entirely ceases.

It is at this season of the year that the large floats of timber come down with the rising of the waters from the hills.

The most unhealthy month of the year is September, the close of the rains. Fever of a bad type is then very prevalent. In the months of April and May the epidemics of small-pox and cholera make their appearance, ceasing at the commencement of the rains. The prevalent wind during the rains and hot season is from the south-west. An easterly wind, if of long continuance, is said to be unhealthy. In the cold season the wind generally comes from the north. At the commencement and breaking up of the rains, violent storms of thunder and lightning occur.

Where the hills rise to any considerable height, they become rocky and precipitous, the lower ranges being composed generally of sand or a rich loam. The dark-brown rocks, of which the higher ranges are composed, are undoubtedly of igneous origin; indeed subterranean volcanic force must at some remote period have caused the strange bellowy upheaval of the face of the country, which gives it its present distinctive character. On the 2nd of April, 1762, Chittagong was violently shaken by an earthquake, the earth opening in many places, and throwing up water and mud of a sulphureous smell. At a place called Bardavun a large river was dried up; and at Bakur Chunak, near the sea, a tract of ground sank down, and 200 people, with all their cattle, were lost. Unfathomable chasms are described as remaining open in many places after the shocks; and villages, some of which subsided several cubits, were overflown with water, among others, Deepgoung, which was submerged to the depth of 7 cubits. Two volcanoes are said to have opened in the Seeta Cúnda Hills. The shock was also felt at Calcutta[4]. There are at present in the Seetakoond Range, in the Chittagong District, several hot springs, from one

[4] Lyall's Geology, vol. ii. ch. xvi. p. 250; Dodsley's Ann. Regist. 173; Phil. Trans. vol. liii.

of which an inflammable gas rises in such quantity, that it is kept constantly burning over the spring. I have heard also of hot springs existing in the Loongshem Range in this District, but I have not visited them. Salt licks are found at many places in the hills; the best known are those at Bhang-a-mora, in the north, and Mawdang Tlang, in the eastern part of the district.

Lignite is found at two or three places in the hills, but no coal has as yet been discovered. An inferior species of lime-stone is found in two places; on being burnt, however, it has not given a return sufficient to render its manufacture profitable.

In many parts of the district are found large and richly alluvial plains, covered for the most part with forest trees. These plains, if cleared of timber, would be found admirably adapted for plough cultivation. Far in the jungles on the banks of the Myannee, an affluent of the Kassalong River, are found tanks, fruit-trees, and the remains of masonry buildings,—evidence that, at some by-gone period, the land here was cultivated and inhabited by men of the plains. Tradition attributes these ruins to a former Rajah of Hill Tipperah, who, it is said, was driven from that part of the country by hordes of hill men coming from the south. At one place only in the hills, at Rangamuttee, on the Kurnafoolee River, has the usual method of cultivation by the plough been introduced; and there are there about 120 families of Bengallees who till the land. The settlement, although established some six years ago, does not appear to have increased either in numbers or in the area of land brought under cultivation. Along the whole border of the district adjacent to Chittagong the narrow glens and small patches of low land have been cultivated by the Bengallees; but the men of the plains have an invincible objection to enter the hills. They are, I believe, principally deterred from settling there by the insalubrity of the climate, which seems to be deadly to their race, although innocuous to the hill men.

There are at present no roads in the district; the nature of the country, indeed, with its transverse ranges of hills, offers very great engineering obstacles to the construction of roads or the employment of wheel-carriage. Paths there are, of course, in every direction; but, with the exceptions to be mentioned hereafter, only such paths as the people of the country can make use of. The favourite path throughout the district is the sandy bed of a stream, as it offers coolness for the feet and shade from the umbrageous canopy of jungle overhead. In crossing a hill range, however, this sort of path necessarily becomes of a precipitous, not to say break-neck, description.

During the last few years a line of paths has been cut through the jungle, connecting the Government frontier guard-posts and the three principal stations in the Hill Tracts: these paths, however, are cut chiefly with a view to military defensive operations, and are not much used as yet by the country people. There are four bazaars or markets in the hills, to which the hill people resort to barter their produce for such articles of daily consumption as salt, spices, dried fish, and the like, which are only procurable from the plains. These bazaars are situated at Kassalong, Rangamuttee, and Chandragoona, on the Kurnafoolee, and at Bundrabun, on the River Sungoo. The bazaar at Chandragoona derives a fictitious importance from that place being at present the head-quarters of the district; but should the central station be at any time removed, the bazaar would collapse, the position occupied not being a true mercantile centre, and the bazaar, moreover, being brought into a competition which it is unable to sustain with the adjacent market of Rangonea, which is an old-established place of barter, much resorted to by the hill population [5].

The population of the hills also resort to such of the markets of the plains as may be

[5] The question of the transfer of the district head-quarters from Chandragoona to Rangamuttee is at present under the consideration of the Bengal Government.

within a day's journey from their homes, along the border of the Chittagong District.

The hill men bring down for sale cotton and timber, either in the rough or hewn into boats; and if much pressed for money, they collect for sale the oil-bearing seeds of a tree in the jungle (*chal mongree*), or cut and float down a raft of bamboos. They also occasionally bring in for sale ivory and wax in small quantities. The principal articles disposed of to the hill people in the bazaars are salt, tobacco (in small quantities), piece goods, metal goods, trinkets, dried fish, pigs, and cattle. About 50,000 cubic feet of timber per annum, it is calculated, is brought down yearly to the plains from the Hill Tract forests; and 55,854 maunds of cotton are estimated to be yearly exported by the hill people,—this in addition to the not inconsiderable quantity reserved by them for home consumption. The Hill Tracts, indeed, seem peculiarly well fitted, both in soil and climate, for the production of cotton. The quantity produced, however, depends almost entirely upon the amount of rain-fall. Too heavy a fall of rain spoils the cotton crop; there is especial danger of this at the commencement of the rains, when the plants are young. Measures have been taken to introduce improved varieties of the cotton plant among the hill tribes. The Flora of the Hill Tracts is of the Malayan type; the forests being principally of brilliant, glossy evergreen trees.

Throughout the whole district are found large tracts of valuable forest trees. Teak is not indigenous, but thrives if planted; it grows, however, plentifully in the forests on the other side of the hill range separating this district from Arracan. A large trade in railway-sleepers has lately sprung up from the port of Chittagong; the Port Conservator estimates that upwards of 30,000 sleepers have been exported during the last two years.

As yet no organized inquiry into the vegetable products of this part of the country has ever been instituted, and but little, consequently, is known on the subject. The tea plant is believed to be indigenous in the district, but it has not hitherto been found in abundance. The fir-tree and the caoutchouc tree are found in the lofty hills in the east of the district; but the hitherto unsatisfactory relations existing between us and the more remote hill tribes have prevented any use being made of these otherwise valuable forest products.

In the wilder parts of the district the forest trees are festooned with numerous ligneous creepers (*phytocrene*) hanging in a labyrinth of coils from every tree; some are as thick as a man's arm. On cutting one of these, water is obtained; and as they grow on the loftiest hill where water is often not obtainable, this property of theirs is most useful. The most curious thing is, that should the coil be cut in one place only, so as to leave two pendent ends, no water issues. It is necessary to cut a piece clean out of the creeper with two quick, consecutive strokes, before water is obtained. If with an unskilled hand three or four hacks are made before severing it, the only result is a dry stick. Two speedy cuts, however, and from the piece of creeper trickles out about half a tumbler full of clear, cool water. The hill men explain this by saying that when the stem is cut the water tries to run away upwards.

There is also a tree in the jungles called "chowr" by the Bengallees, and "samul" in the Tipperah tongue. The young shoots of this tree are delicious eating, being white and tender, with a filbert flavour. Between the outer husk and the trunk of this tree is a soft layer of substance that makes an excel-lent tinder.

In shady spots is also found another edible plant, something like asparagus; the Ben-gallees call it "tara." It is cultivated as a vegetable by the Bengallees, but the wild variety growing in the virgin soil of undis-turbed forests is far superior. The young shoots of the cane and bamboo, just as the young plant emerges from the earth, are very good eating. On the hills, also, the wild yam is found plentifully, so that no man able to search for food in the jungles could starve in these hills.

The hill people have many plants and simples which they use medicinally. They make two or three dyes from the roots and leaves of plants. They also use a certain creeper in catching fish; this plant, when steeped in a stream, and the water confined by a dam, has the property of intoxicating and stupefying the fish, which come floating, belly upwards, to the surface of the water, and are then easily caught.

There are eleven varieties of the bamboo found throughout the hills, and canes grow in profusion. The cane is the hill man's rope; with it he weaves baskets, binds his house together, and throws bridges over the otherwise impassable hill torrents.

The bamboo is literally his staff of life. He builds his house of the bamboo; he fertilizes his fields with its ashes; of its stem he makes vessels in which to carry water; with two bits of bamboo he can produce fire; its young and succulent shoots provide a dainty dinner dish; and he weaves his sleeping mat of fine slips thereof. The instruments with which his women weave their cotton are of bamboo. He makes drinking-cups of it, and his head at night rests on a bamboo pillow; his forts are built of it; he catches fish, makes baskets and stools, and thatches his house with the help of the bamboo. He smokes from a pipe of bamboo; and from bamboo ashes he obtains potash. Finally, his funeral pile is lighted with bamboo. The hill man would die without the bamboo, and the thing he finds hardest of credence is that in other countries the bamboo does not grow, and that men live in ignorance of it. Throughout the whole of India, indeed, the bamboo occupies a forward place in the domestic economy of the inhabitants. It remained only that it should be deified; and this, it seems, has been done. In Dr. Balfour's account of the migratory tribes of Central India (J. A. S., No. 61 of 1844), he tells of a tribe called the Bhatos, a tribe who follow the profession of athletæ, and perform most of their feats with the aid of a bamboo.

"Their patron goddess is Korewa, an incarnation of Mahadeva. Her shrine is situated at the village of Thekoor, near Kittoor, around which dense forests of bamboos grow. One they select, and the attendants of the temple consecrate it. It is now called 'gunnichari,' or chief, and receives their worship annually. To it, as to a human chief, all respect is shown; and in cases of marriage, of disputes requiring arbitration, or the occurrence of knotty points demanding consultation, the 'gunnichari' is erected in the midst of the counsellors or arbiters, and all prostrate themselves to it before commencing the discussion of the subject before them." This is certainly the best kind of chief I ever heard of.

In like manner, one of the clans in the Hill Tracts (the Riang Tipperahs) offer worship to the bamboo. They do not, however, go the length of the Bhatos, in considering it as a chief, for it is to them merely an impersonation or representative of the deity of the forest.

The mode of cultivation pursued in the hills is common to all the tribes; indeed, wherever hill tribes are found throughout India, this special mode of cultivating the earth seems to prevail. It is known as "toung-ya" in Burmah and Arracan, as "dhai-ya" in the Central Provinces, while here the method is usually called "joom," and the hill men pursuing it "joomahs." The *modus operandi* is as follows:—In the month of April, a convenient piece of forest land is fixed upon, generally on a hill-side, the luxuriant under-growth of shrubs and creepers has to be cleared away, and the smaller trees felled: the trees of larger growth are usually denuded of their lower branches, and left standing. If possible, however, the joomah fixes upon a slope thickly covered with a bamboo jungle of the species called "dolloo;" this, compared with a dense tree jungle, is easy to cut, and its ashes, after burning, are of greater fertilizing power. Although the clearing of a patch of dense jungle is no doubt very severe labour, yet the surroundings of the labourer render his work pleasurable in comparison with the toilsome and dirty task of the cultivators of the plains. On the one hand, the hill man works in the shade of the jungle that he is cutting; he is on a lofty eminence, where every breeze reaches and refreshes him; his spirits are enlivened and his labour lightened by the beautiful prospect stretching out before him: while the rich and varied scenery of the forest stirs his mind above a monotone. He is surrounded by his comrades; the scent of the wild thyme and the buzzing of the forest bee are about him; the young men and maidens sing to their work, and the laugh and joke goes round as they sit down to their mid-day meal under the shade of some great mossy forest tree.

On the other hand, consider the moiling toil of the cultivator of the plains. He maunders along with pokes and anathemas at the tail of a pair of buffaloes, working mid-leg in mud; around him stretches an uninterrupted vista of muddy rice land; there is not a bough or a leaf to give him shelter from the blazing noon-day sun. His women are shut up in some cabin, jealously surrounded by jungle; and if he is able to afford a meagre meal during the day, he will munch it *solus*, sitting beside his muddy plough; add to this, that by his comparatively pleasurable toil, the hill man can gain two rupees for one which the wretched ryot of the plains can painfully earn, and it is not to be wondered at that the hill people have a passion for their mode of life, and regard with absolute contempt any proposal to settle down to the tame and monotonous cultivation of the dwellers in the lowlands.

The joom land once cleared, the fallen jungle is left to dry in the sun, and in the month of May it is fired; this completes the clearing. The firing of the jooms is sometimes a source of danger, as at that season of the year the whole of the surrounding jungle is as dry as tinder, and easily catches fire.

In this way sometimes whole villages are destroyed, and people have lost their lives. I have myself seen a whole mountain-side on fire for four days and four nights, having been ignited by joom-firing. It was a magnificent sight, but such a fire must cause incalculable injury to the forest: young trees especially would be utterly destroyed. Generally, however, by choosing a calm day, and keeping down the fire at the edges of the joom, by beating with boughs, the hill people manage to keep the firing within certain prescribed limits. A general conflagration, such as I have mentioned, is of quite exceptional occurrence.

If the felled jungle has been thoroughly dried, and no rain has fallen since the joom was cut, this firing will reduce all, save the larger forest trees, to ashes, and burn the soil to the depth of an inch or two. The charred trees and logs previously cut down remain lying about the ground; these have to be dragged off the joom, and piled up all round; and with the addition of some brush-wood form a species of fence to keep out wild animals.

Work is now at a stand-still, till the gathering of the heavy clouds and the grumbling of thunder denote the approach of the rains. These signs at once bring a village into a state of activity; men and women, boys and girls, each bind on the left hip a small basket filled with the mixed seeds of cotton, rice, melons, pumpkins, yams, and a little Indian corn; each takes a "daô[6]" in hand, and in a

[6] The "daô" is the hill knife, used universally throughout the country. It is a blade about eighteen inches long, narrow at the haft, and square and broad at the tip; pointless, and sharpened on one side only. The blade is set in a handle of wood; a bamboo root is considered the best. The fighting "daô" is differently shaped; this is a long pointless sword, set in a wooden or ebony handle; it is very heavy, and a blow of almost incredible power can be given by one of these weapons. With both the fighting and the ordinary daô one can make but two cuts; one from the right shoulder downwards to the left, one from the left foot upwards to the right. The reason of this is, that in sharpening the blade, one side only gives the edge, slanting to the other straight face of the blade. Any attempt to cut in a way contrary to those mentioned causes the daô to turn in

short time every hill-side will echo to the "hoiya," or hill call, (a cry like the Swiss jodel,) as party answers party from the paths winding up each hill side to their respective patches of cultivation. Arrived at the joom, the family will form a line, and steadily work their way across the field. A dig with the blunt square end of the daô makes a narrow hole about three inches deep; into this is put a small handful of the mixed seeds, and the sowing is completed. If shortly afterwards the rain falls they are fortunate, and

the hand on the striker, and I have seen some bad wounds inflicted in this manner. The weapon is identical with the "parang latok" of the Malays. The ordinary hill daô is generally stuck naked into the waistband on the right hip, but the fighting daô is provided with a scabbard, and worn at the waist. The daô to a hill man is a possession of great price. It is literally the bread winner; with this he cuts his joom and builds his houses; without its aid the most ordinary operations of hill life could not be performed. It is with the daô that he fashions the women's weaving tools; with the daô he fines off his boat; with the daô he notches a stair in the steep hill-side leading to his joom; and to the daô he frequently owes his life, in defending himself from the attacks of wild animals.

have judged the time well; or (unparalleled luck) if they get wet through with the rain as they are sowing, great will be the jollification on the return home, this being an omen that a bumper season may be expected.

The village now is abandoned by every one, and the men set to work to build a house, each in his own joom, for the crop must be carefully watched to preserve it from the wild pig and deer, which would otherwise play havoc among the young shoots of the rice. The jooms of the whole village are generally situated in propinquity; a solitary joom is very rare. During the rains mutual help and assistance in weeding the crop is given; each one takes his turn to help in his neighbour's joom; no hoeing is done; the crop has merely to be kept clear from weeds by hand labour, and an ample return is obtained. If the rain be excessive, however, the cotton crop is liable to be spoilt, as the young plants die from too much water.

The first thing to ripen is Indian corn; this is about the end of July. Next come the melons, of which there are two or three sorts grown in the jooms; afterwards vegetables of all sorts become fit for gathering; and finally, in September, the rice and other grain ripens. At this time the monkeys and jungle fowl are the chief enemies of the crop. In the month of October the cotton crop is gathered last of all, and this concludes the harvest. The rice having been cut, is beaten from the ear in the joom: it is afterwards rolled up in rough straw-covered bales and carried to the granary in the village.

The country suffers sometimes severely from the visitations of rats. They arrive in swarms, and sweep every thing before them: they eat up the standing corn and empty the granaries of the hill people—nothing stops them. They are said to come from the south, and, strange to say, disappear as suddenly as they make their appearance. The hill folk gravely assured me that during the last visitation, which occurred in 1864, the rats were transformed into jungle fowl; in proof of this, they point out a peculiar draggling feather in the tails of the jungle fowl, which they assert to be a rat's tail.

Besides grain and cotton, the hill tribes grow tobacco. This is planted principally in small valleys on the banks of the hill streams.

The best tobacco is grown in the country near the Matamoree River.

Throughout the whole of the Hill Tracts I know no single instance of a hill man cultivating with the plough: indeed, it is rare to find a man earning his livelihood in any other way save by joom culture. Near the villages of some of the chiefs a few acres of plough-cultivated land may sometimes be seen; this, however, is invariably tended by Bengallee servants engaged for the purpose. The forest conservancy restrictions lately introduced will, however, it is thought, induce many of the hill population to settle down as plough cultivators.

In the country adjacent to the Fenny, where, in consequence of constant jooming, jungle had wholly disappeared, and grass taken its place, the attempt was once before made with every prospect of success : owing to their fear of the independent tribes, the people of that part of the country were unable to move to fresh joom land further eastward, and their own country was thoroughly exhausted from over-cultivation; but they steadfastly held aloof from the plough, preferring to earn a precarious subsistence by the cutting and selling of bamboos and the hewing out of boats. Some few of them, who had or could borrow a small amount of capital, took up the profession of itinerant traders; while others earned or added to their means of livelihood by rearing and herding cattle, for which the country afforded ample pasturage.

The independent tribes have now, however, become quiet, and the people of the Fenny have since then steadily moved to the eastward, and occupied fresh joom land.

The villages of the hill people are formed chiefly by communities composed of persons connected either by blood or marriage. The site of the village is changed as often as the spots fit for cultivation in the vicinity are exhausted. Land once joomed cannot be re-cultivated for a period of eight to ten years, as in less than that time a sufficient growth of jungle does not spring up to give the necessary coating of fertilizing ashes, without which the joom crops would yield but a poor return. They do not seem to be acquainted with the method of terrace cultivation pursued in the Himalayas; indeed the slope of the hills in most parts is so steep, that it is doubtful whether this mode of cultivation would be practicable.

I have sometimes met a hill community as they were changing their residence: long files of men, women, and children, every soul of the village, in fact, proceed to their new place of abode, each one with a long circular basket slung at their backs and supported by a broad strip of soft bark passing over the forehead: each family accompanied by a numerous tribe of the very curly-tailed black hill dog. In some of the baskets are their household goods; in others, a child and a young pig sleep contentedly together. In the old village they have left behind, perhaps, half their property, and this without fear, as there are no thieves in the hills. One of these deserted villages presents a curious spectacle; there are all the evidences of occupation and recent life, but every living creature has disappeared. Granaries may be seen half full of grain: large wooden mortars for pounding the grain, the weaving implements of the women, and some half-finished clothes, all left behind for them to take away at their leisure. They have gone probably a long distance (two days' journey) to the new site of the village; and on arriving there, every family has to build its own house.

Each tribe in the hills has a different way of building; and of this I shall speak further, when referring to the distinctive peculiarities of each tribe. Our own tributary hill tribes all build their houses of bamboo, raised from the ground about ten feet, on bamboo supports, with numerous smaller bamboo props supporting the floor, the roof, and the walls, in every conceivable direction. The floor and walls are made of bamboo split and flattened out; the numerous crevices give free access to every breeze, and render a hill house one of the coolest and most pleasant of habitations. The roof is also of bamboo cross-pieces, thatched with palmyra, or "attop" leaves, called by the Bengallees "krook pata." This forms an impervious and lasting roof, which need only be renewed once in three years, whereas the ordinary grass-thatched roof has to be repaired every year. A hill house perched in an exposed position on the ridge or spur of a lofty eminence looks the frailest structure in the world; its strength, however, is surprising, and in spite of the fearful tempests that sometimes sweep over the hills, I never heard of a house having fallen or being injured by the wind.

The domesticated animals of the hill people are the "guyal," the cow, buffalo, goat, dog, cat, pig, and the common fowl.

The four last-named animals are common to the whole district. Long-haired varieties of the cat, dog, and goat, are found among the independent tribes. The guyal, also, are rarely found with any tribe save those that are independent of our authority. The cow and buffalo are principally found among the people inhabiting the Fenny River country, as that part of the district offers the greatest advantages for pasturage.

One of the most marked peculiarities of the Hill Tract forests is their silence. There would seem to be but few wild animals in the hills, numerically speaking. I have travelled for miles in the wildest part of the district without seeing fur or feather: almost every species of wild animal, however, is found in the hills; and to be a good and successful hunter is a great merit in the eyes of the tribes.

The gibbon monkey (hooluq) is found throughout the hills, and towards the south on the coast the fisher monkey (simia synomolgus) is met with. The lemur is also not unfrequently met with. There are also the small common monkey, which, in large flocks, does dire mischief to the standing crops of the hill men, and a long-tailed white-whiskered variety,—the lungoor. The flying fox (pteropus edulis), the horse-shoe bat, and the small house-bat or flitter mouse, are all found in the hills; also the musk-rat, the badger, the Malay black bear, and several species of wild cats. Tigers are not uncommon, but they do not do much harm. The wild dog is said to be met with, but I have not seen it. The mongoose, the large dark-brown squirrel, the red squirrel, the yellow-bellied variety, the field rat, the bamboo rat, and the porcupine (histrix leucorus), are all more or less frequently met with. The elephant and the Assam rhinoceros are common. The former roam in large herds of 100 to 150 all over the district. The double-horned Sumatran species of rhinoceros was formerly thought not to be a native of this part of the country, but a specimen has recently been captured alive, and brought to Chittagong by Captain Hood, of the Elephant Khedda Department. It was smooth-skinned and unmistakably two-horned. A small, black species of hog is found throughout the district, as also the barking deer, the muntjak, and samber; guyal and wild buffalo are not uncommon. Of birds we have the following varieties:—the beemra (edolius remifer), shrikes, the bulbul, warblers, the water-wagtail, hoopoe koel, the carrion crow (this bird is found largely along the western frontier, but ceases entirely on going far east), minah, hornbill (buceros cavatus), small green parrots, a large blue king-fisher with a red neck, a small variety of the same species, the night-jar, the anvil bird, the peacock, Argus pheasant, the matoora or Arracan pheasant, the button quail, jungle fowl, green pigeon, the large wood-pigeon, ring-dove, kites, fish-eagles, and a few wild duck and snipe. I have seen one partridge, but they are very rarely found in the district. The boa-constrictor is common, and is found of enormous size. Several kinds of poisonous snakes are also met with.

The hills and sea-board of Chittagong, until the rise and consolidation of British authority, were the border-land upon which several races struggled for supremacy. Arracanese, Moguls, and Portuguese all preceded us as masters of the country; and all have left behind them traces of their former supremacy. Bernier's travels and the Seer-ul-Mutâkher-ein give some curious glimpses of the state of affairs in this part of the world previous to the advent of the English.

One extract from Bernier, in particular, from its style and vividness of detail, I think worthy of excerpt here, thus :—

"I shall now bring before the notice of my readers Aurungzebe's uncle, Shaista Khan, who, as I have already said, contributed in an essential degree, by his eloquence and intrigues, to the exaltation of his nephew. He was appointed, as we have seen, Governor of Agra a short time before the battle of Kedgwâ, when Aurungzebe quitted the capital to meet Sultan Suja. He was afterwards nominated Governor of the Deccan and Commander-in-Chief of the forces in that province, and, upon Emir-Jemla's decease, was transferred to the Government of Bengal, appointed General of the army in that kingdom, and elevated to the rank of Mir-ul-omrah, which had become vacant by the death of Jemla.

"It is due to Shaista's reputation to relate the important enterprise in which he was engaged soon after his arrival in Bengal,—an enterprise rendered the more interesting by the fact that it was never undertaken by his great predecessor, for reasons which remain unknown.

The narrative will elucidate the past and present state of the kingdoms of Bengal and Arracan, which have hitherto been left in much obscurity, and will throw light on other circumstances which are deserving of attention.

"To comprehend the nature of the expedition meditated by Shaista, and form a correct idea of the occurrences in the Gulf of Bengal, it should be mentioned that the kingdom of Arracan, or Mugh, has contained during many years several Portuguese settlers, a great number of Christian slaves, or half-caste Portuguese, and other Europeans collected from various parts of the world. That kingdom was the place of retreat for fugitives from Goa, Ceylon, Cochin, Malacca, and other settlements in India, held formerly by the Portuguese, and no persons were better received than those who had deserted their monasteries, married two or three wives, or committed other great crimes. These people were Christians only in name; the lives led by them in Arracan were most detestable; massacring and poisoning one another without compunction or remorse, and sometimes assassinating even their priests, who, to confess the truth, were too often no better than their murderers.

"The King of Arracan, who lived in perpetual dread of the Moguls, kept these foreigners as a species of advanced guard for the protection of his frontier, permitting them to occupy a sea-port, called Chittagong, and making them grants of land. As they were unawed and unrestrained by the Government, it was not surprising that these runagates pursued no other trade than that of rapine and piracy. They scoured the neighbouring seas in light gallies called galliasses, entered the numerous arms and canals of the Ganges, ravaged the islands of Lower Bengal, and often penetrating forty or fifty leagues up the country, surprised and carried away the entire population of villages on market days—and at times, when the inhabitants were assembled for the celebration of a marriage or some other festival. The marauders made slaves of their unhappy captives, and burnt whatever could not be removed. It is owing to these repeated depredations that we see so many fine islands in the mouth of the Ganges, formerly thickly peopled, now entirely deserted by human beings, and become the desolate receptacles of tigers and wild beasts.

"Their treatment of the slaves thus obtained was most cruel; and they had the audacity to offer for sale, in the places which they had but recently ravaged, the aged people whom they could turn to no better account. It was usual to see young persons, who had saved themselves by timely flight, endeavouring to-day to redeem the parent who had been made captive yesterday. Those who were not disabled by age the pirates either kept in their service, training them up to the love of robbery and practice of assassination, or sold to the Portuguese of Goa, Ceylon, St. Thomas, and other places. Even the Portuguese of Hooghly, in Bengal, purchased without scruple these wretched captives, and the horrid traffic was transacted in the vicinity of the island of Galles, near Cape Das Palmas. The pirates, by a mutual understanding, waited for the arrival of the Portuguese, who bought whole cargoes at a cheap rate; and it is lamentable to reflect that other Europeans, since the decline of the Portuguese power, have pursued the same flagitious commerce with the pirates of Chittagong, who boast that they convert more Hindoos to Christianity in a twelvemonth than all the Missionaries in India do in ten years,—a strange mode thus of propagating our holy religion by the constant violation of its most sacred precepts, and by the open contempt and defiance of its most awful sanctions.

"The Portuguese established themselves at Hooghly under the auspices of Jehan Guire, the grandfather of Aurungzebe.

"That prince was free from all prejudice against Christians, and hoped to reap great benefit from their commerce. The new settlers also engaged to keep the Gulf of Bengal clear of pirates. Shah Jehan, a more rigid Mussulman than his father, visited the Portuguese at Hooghly with a terrible punishment. They provoked his displeasure by the encouragement afforded to the depredators of Arracan, and by their refusal to release the numerous slaves in their service, who had all of them been subject to the Moguls. He first exacted, by threats and persuasions, large sums of money from the Portuguese, and when they refused to comply with his ultimate demands, he besieged and took possession of the town, and commanded that the whole population should be transferred as slaves to Agra.

"The misery of these people is unparalleled in the history of modern times; it nearly resembled the grievous captivity of Babylon, for even the children, priests, and monks, shared the universal doom. The handsome women, as well married as single, became inmates of the seraglio; those of a more advanced age or of inferior beauty were distributed among the Omrahs; little children underwent the rite of circumcision, and were made pages; and the men of adult age, allured for the most part by fair promises, or terrified by the daily threat of throwing them under the elephant's feet, renounced the Christian faith; some of the monks remained faithful to their creed, and were conveyed to Goa, and other Portuguese settlements by the kind exertions of the Jesuits and Missionaries at Agra, who, notwithstanding the calamity, continued their dwelling, and were enabled to accomplish their benevolent purpose by the powerful aid of money, and the warm intercession of their friends.

"Before the catastrophe at Hooghly, the Missionaries had not escaped the resentment of Shah Jehan. He ordered the large and handsome church at Agra, which, together with one at Lahore, had been erected during the reign of Jehan Guire, to be demolished. A high steeple stood upon this church, with a bell, whose sound was heard in every part of the city. Some time before the capture of Hooghly, the pirates made a formal offer to the Viceroy of Goa to deliver the whole kingdom of Arracan into his hand. Bastian Consalvez was then Chief of the pirates, and so celebrated and powerful was he, that he married the King of Arracan's daughter. It is said that the Viceroy was too arrogant and envious to listen to this proposal, and felt unwilling that the King of Portugal should be indebted to a man of low origin for so important an acquisition. There was nothing, however, in the proposal to excite surprise, being consonant with the general conduct of the Portuguese in

Japan, Pegu, Ethiopia, and other places. The decay of their power in India is fairly ascribable to their misdeeds, and may be considered, as they candidly allow, a proof of the Divine displeasure. Formerly their name was a tower of strength; and all the Indian princes courted their friendship, and the Portuguese were distinguished for courage, generosity, zeal, religion, immensity of wealth, and the splendour of their exploits; but they were not then, like the Portuguese of the present day, addicted to every vice and to every low and grovelling enjoyment.

"The parties, about the time of which I am speaking, made themselves masters of the island of Sandiva,—an advantageous port commanding part of the mouth of the Ganges. On this spot the notorious Fra Joan, an Augustine monk, reigned as a petty sovereign during many years, having contrived, by what means is unknown, to rid himself of the Governor of the islands.

"These also are the identical freebooters who, as we have seen, repaired in their galliasses to Dacca for the purpose of conveying Sultan Suja to Arracan. They found means of opening some of his chests, and robbing him of many precious stones, which were offered secretly for sale at Arracan, and disposed of for a mere trifle. The diamonds all got into the hands of the Dutch and other Europeans, who easily persuaded the ignorant thieves that the stones were soft, and consequently of no real and intrinsic value.

"I have said enough to give an idea of the trouble, vexation, and expense to which the Mogul was for many years exposed by the unjust and violent proceedings of the pirates established in Arracan. He had always been under the necessity of guarding the inlets of the kingdom of Bengal, of keeping large bodies of troops and a fleet of galliasses on the alert. All these precautions, however, did not prevent the ravaging of his territories; the pirates were become so bold and skilful, that with four or five galliasses they would attack and generally capture or destroy fourteen or fifteen of the Mogul's galleys.

"The deliverance of Bengal from the cruel and incessant devastations of these barbarians was the immediate object of the expedition contemplated by Shaista Khan upon his appointment to the goal of that kingdom. But he had an ulterior design, that of attacking the King of Arracan, punishing him for his cruelty to Sultan Suja and family. Aurungzebe was determined to avenge the murder of those illustrious personages, and, by a single example, to teach his neighbours that the princes of his blood, in all situations and under all circumstances, must be treated with humanity and reverence.

"The Governor of Bengal accomplished his first plan with consummate address. It was scarcely practicable to march an army into the kingdom of Arracan, owing to the great number of rivers and canals that intersect the frontier; and the naval superiority of the pirates rendered it still more difficult to transport an invading force by sea. It therefore occurred to Shaista to apply to the Dutch for their co-operation; and, with this view, he sent an envoy to Batavia, with power to negotiate, on certain conditions, with the General-Commandant of that colony, for the joint occupation of the kingdom of

Arracan, in the same manner as Shah Abas treated formerly with the English in regard to Ormus.

"The Governor of Batavia was easily persuaded to enter into a scheme that offered an opportunity of still further depressing the Portuguese influence in India, and from the success of which the Dutch Company would derive important advantages. He despatched two ships of war to Bengal for the purpose of facilitating the conveyance of the Mogul's troops to Chittagong; but Shaista, in the meantime, had collected a large number of galliasses and other vessels of considerable tonnage, and threatened to overwhelm the pirates in irremediable ruin if they did not immediately submit to the Mogul's authority. 'Aurungzebe is fixed in the resolution,' said he to them, 'of chastising the King of Arracan, and a Dutch fleet, too powerful to be resisted, is near at hand. If you are wise, your personal safety and the care of your families will now engross all your attention, you will quit the service of the King of Arracan and enter into that of Aurungzebe. In Bengal you shall have as much land allotted as you may deem necessary, and your pay shall be double that which you at present receive.'

"The pirates about this period had assassinated one of the King of Arracan's principal officers, and it is not known whether they were more struck with terror by the punishment awaiting them for that crime, or moved by the promises and threats contained in Shaista's communication. Certain it is, however, that these unworthy Portuguese were one day seized with so strange a panic as to embark in forty or fifty galliasses, and sail over to Bengal; and they adopted this measure with so much precipitation that they had scarcely time to take their families and valuable effects on board.

"Shaista received these extraordinary visitors with open arms; gave them large sums of money; provided the women and children with excellent accommodation in the town of Dacca; and after he had thus gained their confidence, the pirates evinced an eagerness to act in concert with the Mogul's troops, and shared in the attack and capture of Sandiva, which island had fallen into the hands of the King of Arracan. Meanwhile, the two Dutch ships-of-war made their appearance, and Shaista having thanked the Commanders for their kind intentions, informed them that he had now no need of their services. I saw the vessels in Bengal, and was in company with the officers, who considered the Indian's thanks a poor compensation for the violation of his engagements. In regard to the Portuguese, Shaista treats them, not perhaps as he promised, but certainly as they deserve. He has drawn them from Chittagong; they and their families are in his power; an occasion for their service no longer exists; he considers it, therefore, quite unnecessary to fulfil a single promise. He suffers month after month to elapse without giving them any pay, declaring that they are traitors, in whom it is folly to confide—wretches who have basely betrayed the prince whose bounty they had experienced.

"In this manner Shaista Khan extinguished in Chittagong the power of those Portuguese who had depopulated and ruined the whole of Lower Bengal. Time will show whether his enterprise against the King of Arracan will be crowned with similar success."

The earliest record of our dealings with the hill tribes is a letter from the Chief of Chittagong to the Governor-General, the Honourable Warren Hastings, Esq., dated 10th April, 1777, in which he reports that "a mountaineer, named Ramoo Cawn, who pays the Company a small revenue on their cotton farm, has, since my being here, either through ill usage from the revenue farmer, or from a disposition to revolt, for some months past, committed great violence on the Company's landholders, by exacting various taxes and imposing several claims on them with no grounds of authority or legal demand." The letter goes on to state that the writer "was flattered with hopes of securing the person of this said Ramoo Cawn;" but this scheme proved abortive, as the man fled from his usual place of residence.

"He has now assembled men in yet larger bodies," and has called to his aid "large bodies of Kookie men, who live far in the interior parts of the hills, who have not the use of fire-arms, and whose bodies go unclothed." This contumacy on the part of Ramoo Cawn was subsequently met by stopping all supplies, and not allowing the hill people to have access to our bazaars; and these measures appear to have been successful, as we hear no more of this person. Tradition in the hills tells us of such a rising of the Chukma tribe; and with reference to this Ramoo Cawn, or Khan, I am the more disposed to ascribe the disturbance in question to the Chukma tribe, as they alone, of all the hill people, employ a *quasi* Mohammedan nomenclature. The Kookie men, however, referred to, do not appear to have quieted down so quickly, for in November, 1777, we find the Chief of Chittagong addressing Captain Edward Ellesker, commanding the 22nd Battalion of Sepoys, and ordering some men to be sent "for the protection of the inhabitants against some Kookies," and "to assist in making a kheddah."

From the above letters and other sources, I gather that we at that time collected revenue from the hills in the shape of a tax on cotton brought down from the hills, which tax was farmed out to some second party. It is also curious to note that as early as 1777 the Government had established kheddahs, and drew their supply of elephants partly from this district.

The records having reference to our relations with the hill tribes, obtainable in the Government offices at Chittagong, are but scanty and intermittent. The attention of the executive seems to have been principally directed to the administration of the District of Chittagong Proper, and it was only when some lawless outrage or default of tribute payment forced them into notice that mention is made of our frontier tribes. There are, therefore, large gaps in the thread of narrative of by-gone years, when we can only conclude that the tribes were quiet, and the authorities content to let them remain so.

On the 6th May, 1784, Government wrote to Mr. Irwin, the Chief of Chittagong, desiring to have his opinion fully, whether, by lenient measures, the inhabitants of the hills might not be induced to become peaceable subjects and cultivators of the low lands. No practical result, however, ensued, and the tribes do not crop up again until the 21st April, 1829, when Mr. Halhed, Commissioner, writes that he finds that the hill tribes are not subjects, but merely tributaries. "I do not recognize any right on our part to interfere with their internal arrangements. We have no authority in the hills; the payment of the tribute which is trivial in amount in each instance is guaranteed by a third party, resident in our own territory, and who is alone responsible. He derives his own profit from the arrangement under stipulations which have no place in his agreement with us. He is merely an agent, or mooktear, or medium of communication between his constituents and the authorities. He is not the ruler of the clan he represents, and possesses no control over the members of it," &c.

Up to 1829, therefore, we seem to have exercised no direct influence or rule over the hill tribes. The near neighbourhood, however, of a powerful and stable Government naturally brought the chiefs by degrees under our influence, and by the end of the 18th century every leading chief paid to the Chittagong Collector a certain tribute or yearly gift made to purchase the privilege of free trade between the inhabitants of the hills and the men of the plains. These sums were at first fluctuating in amount, but gradually were brought to specified and fixed limits, eventually taking the shape, not of tribute, but of revenue paid to the State.

Until the year 1860 it appears we did not interfere directly with the internal economy of the hills. In that year, however, the independent tribes, known by the generic name of Kookies, committed some murderous outrages on British subjects in the adjacent District of Tipperah. These raids were of so organized a description, and on such a large scale, as to cause well-founded anxiety to Government; and in July, 1860, a Superintendent of Hill Tribes was appointed to the charge of the hills, which were henceforth known by the name of the Hill Tracts of Chittagong. The committal of the raids was clearly brought home to the tribes residing in the north-eastern part of the Hill Tracts, and, accordingly, on the 27th January, 1861, an expedition, under the command of Major Raban, entered the hills, and inflicted punishment on the tribe principally concerned.

The primary object of the appointment of a Hill Superintendent was the supervision of the independent tribes; and for the next few years attention was principally directed to the preservation of the peace of the frontier. In 1867 the official designation of the officer in charge of the district was changed from Superintendent of Hill Tribes to Deputy Commissioner of Hill Tracts, and he was vested with full control of all matters pertaining both to revenue and justice throughout the Hill Tracts. At the same time the district was apportioned into subdivisions, and subordinate officers placed in charge thereof.

A force of 375 men, fully armed, equipped, and officered, has been allotted by Government for the defence of the frontier. The men are principally natives of the hills, and are as yet untried in active service.

The general instructions of Government for the guidance of the Hill Tract authorities (Government of Bengal, Letter No. 3300, dated 20th June, 1860) are comprehensive, and so indicative of the wise and beneficent course of policy which has been pursued towards the hill people, that I venture to give here an abstract thereof, as follows:—

1*st.*—To allow no middle-men between the hill man and the "hakim," all mooktears or attorneys being prohibited from employment in matters between hill man and hill man.

2*nd.*—Simplification of procedure and freedom from expense were attained by directing that equity, guided by the spirit of the law, should be observed, no stamps required, and no costs further than actual and necessary expenses. Justice in fact to be administered in the simplest and most expeditious manner possible.

3*rd.*—The customs and prejudices of the

people to be observed and respected. We are to interfere as little as possible between the chiefs and their tribes.

4th.—The Deputy Commissioner was vested with the full powers of a magistrate, his orders being appealable to the Commissioner of the Division, who also has the final decision of all heinous cases.

Such were the principles of administration as at first set on foot, but subsequently, by degrees, and until within the last two years, there was a perceptible tendency to revert to the Regulation Procedure; attorneys had imperceptibly crept into practice, and an appeal to Calcutta in even minor cases was not uncommon, and this last is the case even now. Every effort, however, is used to check and discourage litigation; and, whenever practicable, cases are referred to the arbitration of village juries, the parties pleading in person before these rough tribunals. From their award there is seldom any appeal or dissatisfaction.

The introduction, indeed, of mooktears

among a people simple and unused to law, is at all times highly inexpedient. Their employment tends to crowd the Courts with petty, vexatious, and disgraceful suits. Nothing is so productive of evil passions as facilities for their gratification. The mooktears tamper with the simplicity and ignorance of the people, and draw them into litigations, in which the sole persons benefited are the mooktears themselves. They thrive by quibbles, quirks, and chicanery, and, like vermin, swarm where there is most corruption. They are to the law what quack doctors are to physic, exciting the malady for the purpose of profiting by the cure, and retarding the case in order to pocket the fees; as also in medicine, when a man has once dabbled in patent medicines and infallible specifics, he is always poisoning himself and others by quack drugs, so in the law an ignorant person who has once been tricked into a lawsuit by one of these crafty empirics, is ever afterwards in a chronic state of dispute and embroilment. During the last two years the employment of mooktears has been discouraged in cases between hill men, and in hill matters which require special and local knowledge of customs and the like; but in appeals before the Commissioner, mooktears are allowed to appear, as the hill men are often ignorant of the language spoken in the plains of Chittagong where the Commissioner's Court is held.

In these hills, also, as in Sonthalia, the crafty Bengallee mahajuns of the plains have wrested the law from its original intent, and turned it into an engine wherewith to reduce the people to a condition of slavery. In an ill-fated hour the hill man borrows a few rupees from some mahajun; he wants the money, either because his crops have failed, or his son is to be married, or for some other reason. He can neither read nor write; consequently the bond in which the transaction is recorded usually binds him to pay some enormous amount of interest, of which he is totally ignorant. Time goes on, the money becomes due, and is generally paid. In the latter case the mahajun says, "Go, my son,

I destroy the bond, the debt is cancelled;" here he will tear up some paper before the hill man, but most certainly *not* the bond. The debtor goes away satisfied to his home, leaving the mahajun chuckling in his sleeve at his successful villany. After a short interval the mahajun repairs to the Civil Court, and, with an injured aspect, lays a suit for the recovery of the original debt, interest, and costs of suit, according to his bond. Formerly, when the summons to the hill man to appear in the suit was issued through a Bengallee peon, the mahajun would simply bribe the summons-bearer, who would report the summons as duly served, without going near the pseudo debtor's house. Should the mahajun not be successful in this, he will lie in wait at the river-side, and when his man comes down on the day fixed for the hearing of the case, he will seize upon him, "Ai! bapré! great is my misfortune, you have been summoned, my friend, quite by mistake; I have no case against you; you know, we made all square between us when last we met. I am afflicted for your trouble, but come with me, you must eat and drink at my expense as some small return for all this needless bother." So off goes the befooled hill man, and never appears in his case, when, according to law, a decree in default is given against him. In another case, supposing the hill man to have paid part of his debt, and to owe the remainder, the mahajun will then meet him outside the Court, make a compromise with him, and agree to withdraw the case. The man goes away, while the mahajun, on his part, does not withdraw the case, but takes a decree in full, *ex parte*, in default of the debtor's attendance. These are not imaginary cases, but have come actually under my own observation. Numberless are the tricks to which the crafty Bengallee resorts, and gradually he accumulates over his victim's head an amount of legally authorized debt, which the wretched creature can never hope to pay off. He then becomes the bond-slave of the mahajun; for him he toils, for his profit he clears a joom, raises cotton, or hews out a boat, and even death does not release him, for the load descends upon the shoulders of his son.

Latterly so many cases came before the Courts, of a nature such that a permanent state of ill feeling between the hill population and the mahajuns was to be apprehended, that it was found necessary to limit both the amount of interest on a debt recoverable by law, and the time during which a decree might be allowed to remain unexecuted. Twelve per cent. per annum is now granted by the Courts, and on a decree being obtained, the creditor is compelled to enforce it at once.

The appointment of an officer for the exclusive supervision of this district has greatly ameliorated the condition of the hill people in this as in other respects, and the special Registration Rules which have been lately introduced have now almost entirely put a stop to the nefarious practices above referred to.

It would be a mistake, in my opinion, to introduce into this district the Regulations, Legal Codes, and Procedure, as followed in other parts of India. Such a measure could not fail to be most unpopular and distasteful to the people at large[7].

Man, in his earliest conditions, in a state of quasi barbarism, is tutored by the elements, and imbibes certain habits and dispositions from the air he breathes and the food he takes.

The hill men like neither the plains nor their inhabitants. Law is, or ought to be, the expression of the popular voice; the measure prescribed and agreed to by the people in general, from time to time, for the safeguard and protection of their lives, liberties, and property: law is the concretion or aggregate of hundreds of years of trial and experiment. We should not, I think, do well to put aside custom and rules[8] which have existed among

[7] The Locrians admitted only two new laws in two hundred years, because he who proposed to establish or change one came with a halter round his neck, and was strangled if his proposition was rejected.

[8] The haste or prejudice which has refused to the rudimentary ideas of justice, on which all Codes are based, all but the most superficial examination, must bear the blame of the unsatisfactory condition in which

the hill people from time immemorial, and supply their place by Codes utterly dissonant to their whole mode of life and thinking. This would not be law, but the tyranny of a strong minority over a simple and ignorant majority. Such a tyranny was that which in ancient times among the Hindoos prescribed mutilation as the penalty for spitting on the robe of a Brahmin[9]. See in Bengal, a wealthy Zemindar is put in jail for bribery, or here in these hills a Chief is punished for keeping slaves or levying what we call an illegal cess on his people: when that Chief or that Zemindar leaves jail, his people will flock round him to do him honour as an injured person. I do not attempt to defend slavery or to infer that

we at present find the science of jurisprudence.—*Maine's Ancient Law*, p. 3.

[9] "If a Soodar (man of low caste) sits upon the carpet of a Brahmin, in that case the Magistrate, having thrust a hot iron into his buttock and branded him, shall banish him the kingdom, or else he shall cut off his buttock. If a Soodar, out of pride, shall spit his phlegm on a Brahmin's body, the Magistrate shall cut off his lip."—*Extracts from the Law of the Gentoos, compiled by Mr. Halhed in* 1775.

bribery should not be put a stop to; I only say that there is no law the infraction of which carries with it no social penalty.

The revenue of the Hill Tracts consists chiefly of the tribute which is paid to Government by the chiefs of the tribes. A considerable sum of money is also obtained yearly from the tolls levied on behalf of Government on all spontaneous forest produce brought down by water or river routes to the plains. The fear of the inroads and attacks of the independent tribes on the frontier has hitherto prevented the large level tracts existing all over the district from being occupied and cultivated by Bengallee settlers, but a movement is now commencing, and during the last year or two, much land along the Chittagong border of the district has been leased to men of the plains, and there is but little doubt that under more favourable conditions of tranquillity the greater portion of the district will be brought under cultivation, and that the main source of revenue, as in other parts of India, will arise from the land-tax.

PART II.

THE HILL TRIBES.

The usages which a particular community is found to have adopted in its infancy and in its primitive seats are generally those which are on the whole best suited to promote its physical and moral well-being.—MAINE'S ANCIENT LAW, page 19.

THE tribes that inhabit the Hill Tracts of Chittagong may be named and classified as follows :—

1. The Khyoungtha, or Children of the River, who are of pure Arracanese origin, speaking the ancient Arracan dialect, and conforming in every way to Buddhist customs. Under this head may also be named the Chuckma tribe, for reasons which I shall state hereafter.

2. The Toungtha, or Children of the Hills, who are of mixed origin, if indeed they are not the aboriginal inhabitants of the country. They speak numerous and diversified dialects, and are more purely savages than the Khyoungtha. Under this head are included

the Tipperah and the Lhoosai, or Kookie tribes, with their offshoots.

The word Khyoungtha and Toungtha are both Arracanese:—"Khyoung," a river; "toung," a hill; and "tha," or "tsa," a son. They are used as generic terms, to denote the hill tribes, by only such of our tribes as speak the Arracan dialect. The other tribes have each their own way of specifying themselves and their neighbours, which will be alluded to when speaking of each tribe in particular; but none of them appear to have any general term for all hill dwellers.

The Bengallees distinguish hill men into two classes. The friendly tribes living close along the Chittagong District border they call Joomahs; and all other hill men, more especially if unable to speak the vernacular of Bengal, are distinguished as Kookies.

A greater portion of the hill tribes at present living in the Chittagong Hills undoubtedly came about two generations ago from Arracan. This is asserted both by their own traditions and by records in the Chittagong Collectorate. It was in some measure due to the exodus of our hill tribes from Arracan that the Burmese War of 1824 took place, which ended in the annexation to British territory of the fertile Province of Arracan. As this is a point interesting, not only from its local bearing on the hill tribes, but also in a larger and more important historical sense, I shall trace here the way in which the dissensions between the English authorities and the Burmese, which eventually culminated in war, hinged in a great measure upon refugees from the hill tribes, who, fleeing from Arracan into our territory, were pursued and demanded at our hands by the Burmese.

Among the earliest records that we have of our dealings with the Burmese are two letters, written, one by the King of Burmah, the other by the Rajah of Arracan, to the Chief of Chittagong, and received about the 24th June, 1787, couched as follows :—

"From the Rajah of Arracan to the Chief of Chittagong. Our territories are composed of five hundred and sixty countries, and we have ever been on terms of friendship, and the inhabitants of other countries willingly and freely trade with the countries belonging to each of us. A person named Keoty, having absconded from our country, took refuge in yours. I did not, however, pursue him with a force, but sent a letter of friendship on the subject, desiring that Keoty might be given up to me. You, considering your own power and the extent of your possessions, refused to send him to me. I, also, am possessed of an extensive country; and Keoty, in consequence of his disobedient conduct and the strength and influence of my King's good fortune, was destroyed.

" Domcan Chukma, and Kiecopa Lies, Marring and other inhabitants of Arracan, have now absconded and taken refuge near the mountains within your border, and exercise depredations on the people belonging to both countries; and they, moreover, murdered an Englishman at the mouth of the Naf, and stole away every thing he had with him. Hearing of this, I am come to your boundaries with an army, in order to seize them, because they have deserted their own country, and disobedient to my King, exercise the profession of robbers. It is not proper that you should give asylum to them or the other Mughs who have absconded from Arracan, and you will do right to drive them from your country, that our friendship may remain perfect, and that the road of travellers and merchants may be secured. If you do not drive them from your country and give them up, I shall be under the necessity of seeking them out with an army, in whatever part of your territories they may be. I send this letter by Mahomed Wassene. Upon the receipt of it, either drive the Mughs from your country, or, if you mean to give them an asylum, return me an answer immediately."

This letter is explicit enough. The fugitives referred to are evidently men of the Chuckma and Mrúng hill tribes, who to this day preserve the recollection of their ancestor's flight from Arracan. The persons in question were probably the Chiefs of the clans, and the driving of them from British territory would have been equivalent to the expulsion of the whole clan.

The other letter from the King of Burmah is evidently a covering epistle, from beneath the shelter of which his representative of Arracan should fire his sharp little pop-gun of defiance. His Majesty of the Golden Foot and the White Elephant writes in a broad umbrageous manner, that even to the present day carries with it a sense of comfort to the reader. The missive is most curious and characteristic. I shall therefore give it *in extenso*. It marches in broad epic periods, with a roll as of deep-toned gongs and a barbaric clash of cymbals.

"*Letter from Turboomah, Principal of the Burmese, forwarded by his orders through the head person in charge of the Arracan country.*

"I am lord of a whole people and of one hundred and one countries, and my titles are Rajah Chatterdary (sitting under a canopy) and Rajah Suruj Bunshee (descendant of the sun, and sitting under a splendid canopy of gold). I hold in subjection to my authority many Rajahs. Gold, silver, and jewels, are the produce of my country; and in my hand is the instrument of war, that, as the lightning of heaven, humbles and subdues my adversaries. My troops require neither injunctions nor commands, and my elephants and horses are without number. In my service are ten Pundits, learned in the Shaster, and one hundred and four priests, whose wisdom is not to be equalled, agreeably to whose learning and intelligence I execute and distribute justice among my people, so that my mandates, like the lightning, suffer no resistance or control. My subjects are endowed with virtue and the principles of justice, and refrain from all immoral practices; and I am as the sun, blessed with the light of wisdom to discover the secret designs of men.

"Whoever is worthy of being called a Rajah is merciful and just towards his people. Thieves, robbers, and disturbers of the peace, have at length received the punishment due to their crimes, and now the word of my mouth is dreaded as the lightning from heaven.

"I am as a great sea among two thousand rivers and many nullahs; and I am as the Mountain Shuneroo, surrounded by forty thousand hills, and like unto these is my authority extending itself over one hundred and one Rajahs. Further, ten thousand Rajahs pay daily attendance at my durbar, and my country excels every country in the world. My palace, as the heavens, studded with gold and precious stones, is revered more than any other place in the universe. My occupations resemble the business of the chief angels, and I have written unto all the provinces of Arracan with orders to forward this letter in safety to Chittagong, formerly subject to the Mogul Rajah, by whom the country was cultivated and populated, and who erected twenty-four hundred palaces of public worship, and made four and twenty tanks (here follows a long list of the names of palaces and forts said to have been erected by the above Rajah), and by Umbung Dumah[1], Rajah of Omerpoor. Previous to his accession to the Rajagyee, the country was subject to other Rajahs, whose title was Chattordary (sitting under a canopy), who erected places of worship and appointed priests to administer the rites of religion to people of every denomination (*observe the tolerance of the Buddhist*); but at that period the country was ill governed, previous to the accession of Rajah Serytumah Chuckah to the government of the countries of Ruttenpoor, Doogwady, Arracan, Doorgaputty, Ramputty, Chaydoge, Mahodyne, Manang, in whose time the country was governed with

---

[1] This probably refers to the Rajah of Hill Tipperah, known by the title of Durm, or Joob Rajah. The ancient residence of the Rajah of Hill Tipperah was at a place called Odehpoor.

justice and ability, and his wisdom was a shining light, and the people were happy under his administration. He was also favoured with the friendship of the religious men of the age, one of whom, by name Buddha, resorted to his place of residence, and was solicited by the Rajah to appoint some one for the purpose of instructing him in religious rites; and Thaw-hmarey was accordingly appointed agreeably to the Rajah's requisition.

"At this time it rained from heaven gold, and silver, and precious stones, which were buried underground in charge of the above priest, whose house also was of gold and silver workmanship, to which the people resort and worship the deities; and the Rajah kept a large establishment of servants and of slaves at the temple for the service of travellers and passengers, and his time was engaged in the studying of the five books. He always refrained from immoral practices and deeds interdicted by his religion, and his priests abstained from the flesh of geese, pigeons, goats, hogs, and of fowls; and wickedness and theft, adultery, falsehood, and drinking were unknown in that age.

"I likewise preserve a line of conduct and religion similar to the above; but previous to my conquest of Arracan, the people were as snakes wounding men—a prey to enmity and disorder; and in Magadha, Mayenwong, Darawody, Chagadag Rahmawady there were eaters of the flesh of man, and wickedness prevailed amongst them, so that no man relied upon his neighbours. At this time, one Buddha Dutta, otherwise Seeryboat Thakoor, came down in the country of Arracan, and instructed the people and the beasts of the field in the principles of religion and rectitude; and, agreeably to his word, the country was governed for a period of five thousand years, so that peace and good-will subsisted among them.

"Agreeably hereto is the tenour of my conduct and government of my people; and as there is an oil, the produce of a certain spot of the earth, of exquisite flavour, so is my dignity and power above that of all other Rajahs; and Jafboo, the High Priest, having consulted with others of that class, represented to me, on the 15th of the month Praso 1148, saying, do you enforce the laws and customs of Serryboat Thakoor, which I accordingly did, and, moreover, erected places of divine worship, and have conformed myself strictly to the laws and customs of Sery-Tumah Cuckah, governing my people with lenity and justice.

"As the country of Arracan lies contiguous to Chittagong, if a treaty of commerce were established between me and the English, perfect unity and alliance would ensue from such engagements. I therefore have submitted it to you that the merchants of your country should resort hither for the purpose of purchasing pearls, ivory, wax, and that in return my people should be permitted to resort to Chittagong for the purpose of trafficking in such commodities as the country may afford; but as the Mughs residing at Chittagong have deviated from the principles of religion and morality, they ought to be corrected for their errors and irregularities according to the written laws, insomuch as those invested with power will suffer eternal punishment in case of any deviation from their religion and laws, but whoever conforms his conduct to the strict rules of piety and religion will hereafter be translated to heaven. I have accordingly sent four elephants' teeth, under the charge of thirty persons, who will return with your answer to the above proposals and offers of alliance."

These letters were received during the administration of Lord Cornwallis. They were followed up almost immediately by the entrance into our territory of a force of armed Burmese under the Sirdar of Arracan. The Chief of Chittagong, in the same month of June, writes to the Governor-General in Council, reporting this incursion, and stating that he has declined to respond to the overtures of alliance until this armed force was withdrawn. At the same time he states that in his opinion the refugees should be driven out of British territory. He adds, also, that these fugitives were persons of some consequence in Arracan, and reports, further, that a Chukma Sirdar, who had fled from Arracan, had been arrested and confined by him. He concludes by stating his opinion that this Sirdar and his tribe have no intention of cultivating the low lands in a peaceable manner, but have taken up their abode in the hills and jungles, for the convenience of plundering. Ten years before this, in the year 1777, it appears from a letter dated 31st May, from the Chief of Chittagong to the Honourable Warren Hastings, Governor-General, that some thousands of hill men had come from Arracan into the Chittagong limits, having been offered encouragement to settle by one Mr. Bateman, who was the chief governing officer there at that time. These migrations were evidently for a long time a rankling sore to the Burmese authorities; and Macfarlane's History of British India, page 355, records that in 1795 a Burmese army of 5000 men again pursued some rebellious Chiefs, or, as they called them, robbers, right into the English District of Chittagong. These Chiefs, who had taken refuge in our territories, were eventually given up to the Burmese, and "two out of the three were put to death with atrocious tortures."

In 1809 Macfarlane records that disputes

continued to occur in the frontiers of Chittagong and Tipperah, but the organized forays into our territory hardly assumed any definite form until 1823 (Wilson's Narrative of the Burmese War, page 25), when a rupture ensued, which led to the war of 1824. The primary cause, therefore, of all these disturbances, rendering the Burmese apt to provoke and take offence, was undoubtedly the emigration to our hills of tribes hitherto subject to their authority.

The origin of the tribes is a doubtful point. Pemberton ascribes to them a Malay descent. Colonel Sir A. Phayre considers two of the principal tribes of Arracan, who are also found in these hills, to be of Myamma or Burmese extraction. Among the tribes themselves no record exists, save that of oral tradition, as to their origin. The Khyoungtha alone are possessed of a written language; they have among them several copies of the Raja-wong; or History of the Kings of Arracan, but I have been able to discover no records whatever as to their sojourn and doings in the hills. The Toungtha, on the other hand, possess no written character, and the languages spoken by them are simple to a degree, expressing merely the wants and sensations of uncivilized life. The information obtainable as to their origin and past history is therefore naturally meagre and unreliable.

The general physique of the hill tribes is strongly Mongolian. They are, as a rule, short in stature, about 5 feet 6 inches in height. Their faces are broad; the nose flat, with no perceptible bridge; the eyes narrow, and set obliquely in the head, high cheek bones, and no beard or moustache. They have an honest, bright look, with a frank and merry smile; and their look does not belie them, but is a faithful index of their mental characteristics.

The complexion of the Khyoungtha tribes is a clear yellow or wheaten colour, much resembling the skin colour of the Chinese. The Toungtha however are dark and swarthy in complexion.

Before noticing in detail the peculiarities and distinctive signs of each separate tribe, I shall describe certain habits and customs which are common to all of them :—The first and perhaps the most marked distinction is their mode of cultivation, which has already been described by me; next in importance is the relation of master and servant, or, as we should call it, slavery, throughout the hills[2].

[2] The custom of slavery formerly existed also in the Chittagong District. On this point, the Chief of Chittagong writes to the Honourable Warren Hastings, President in Council, dated September 1st, 1774, as follows: —"I have been duly honoured with your letter of the 4th June and 12th July. Through a multiplicity of business, it has escaped me to acknowledge the receipt of them sooner. However, your order respecting the purchasing of slaves was immediately published, and I have now the pleasure to enclose you a particular account, in English and Persian, of the customs that have hitherto prevailed in this province with respect to the right that masters have over their slaves. The translation enclosed is as follows :—'The custom with respect to slaves in this country is this,—any one who is without a father, mother, or any other relation, and who is not connected with any zemindar or other in the revenue or cultivation of the country, who is destitute of the necessaries of life, and should propose selling himself, on the receipt of the

Servants, as we understand the term, that is, persons doing menial service for a certain wage, there are none; but the universal custom prevailed in the hills, until within the last five years, of having debtor-slaves. Per-

money for which he agrees, becomes a slave; and should his owners ever fall destitute, and be in want of the necessaries of life, they may sell him, her, or them to whomsoever they please, and the purchaser is from that time considered as the master of the slaves. The children, grandchildren, and so on to many generations, become the slaves of their parents' masters, and they must do whatever is ordered, whether to cultivate, build, or any sort of drudgery. Their wives must also attend on the wife of their master. When they marry, it must be to a slave, and that of their master's choosing, who defrays the expense of the wedding; and they can on no account marry without their master's consent. The Province of Islamabad is a small and poor one; there are many people of good families, but poor, whose chief dependence and support is by their slaves, who do every sort of menial service, which a hired servant will not do, through fear of demeaning himself and disgracing his family. The above custom has prevailed time out of mind, and discontinuation of it would cause many unforeseen distresses, innumerable complaints on the part of the masters, and at the same time would not be satisfactory to the slaves, who, owing to usage, have no desire to live otherwise.'"

sons borrowed money from their Chief or some other well-to-do individual, and gave one of their children or a female relative to serve as a menial servant until the debt should be paid or cancelled. This service took the place of interest on the money lent, no interest being payable; but the creditor was bound to release the slave on the repayment or tender of the original sum borrowed. The condition of these so-called slaves was very little different indeed from that of free people. They were treated as members of the creditor's family, and were never exposed to harsh usage. They could not be sold or transferred to another owner. Their position in all cases was far preferable to the galling bondage in which hill men were subsequently often legally held by the Bengallee mahajuns, as already described in Part I. Since we have taken in hand the direct management of the hills, this system has been put down with the strong hand; upwards of three hundred debtor slaves have been released[3]; some at

[3] Colonel Sir A. Phayre, in Asiatic Society's Journal,

the request of their relatives, who wished to get off paying their creditors, others simply because they were supposed to be slaves; many of these latter returned afterwards to their debtors to fulfil their engagements. The Chiefs and principal men, however, being immediately under the eye of authority, were unable to retain in their houses a single menial, and the ordinary daily work of their houses suddenly fell upon their wives and daughters. As a consequence of this measure, confidence between debtor and creditor was

No. 117, page 701, says that slaves among the hill tribes have been emancipated in the adjacent District of Arracan; and adds in a note, "The chiefs complain of this as a very great hardship. In a Khyong tribe I once met a young chief who had lost one of his fingers. It appeared that his slaves had one fine morning absconded, and he was obliged to set to work himself in clearing his forest land. By his clumsiness, he soon cut off a finger; and now he held up his mutilated hand to me in dumb appeal for the restitution of his slaves. This young man was all but naked, and a blush was visible in his clear olive cheek, when the Rakhoingthas with me threw a cloth over him, and he heard, for the first time in his life, that he was committing a breach of decency in appearing unclothed."

shaken. The hill men no longer sought assistance from their Chiefs, or sought it uselessly. They could neither read nor write Bengallee, which was the language of our Courts; and even the ability to speak this alien language was uncommon among them. How then draw up the bond by which only a debt could be legalized? How become acquainted with or comply with the Procedure of Act VIII. of 1859, according to which all suits for debt must be laid?

The consequences of our action being such, the old system under which hill people borrowed from each other in times of need having been rudely overturned, and in its place a law, unexplained and incomprehensible, being substituted, they fell easy victims to the mahajuns, who expounded the law very much to their own advantage. The fault of our measures lay in their suddenness; there was no intermediate stage, although previously in the abolition of slavery in our West Indian Colonies, the measure was there introduced with great caution and by progressive stages.

The slavery in these hills, if, indeed, it can be called slavery, was of the mildest description, and was the deliberately adopted custom of the majority of the people, not a bondage imposed by force. We are, I think, too apt to connect the idea of slavery with the whip, chains, and cruelty; but it should be remembered that in the lower ranks of progress slavery does good work; without it, indeed, civilization would have been well nigh impossible. Slaves exempt man from the otherwise all-powerful necessity of working for his life, from earning bread by the sweat of his brow, and their possession gives leisure for thought and culture. It is not so many centuries ago since even in our own England a modified description of slavery existed; and in the early growth of a people there always has been, and must be, slavery, if they are to rise in the scale of races. Among the hill tribes labour cannot be hired; the people work each one for himself. In 1865, in this district, a road had to be cut; but although fabulous wages were offered, the hill population steadily refused to work, and labourers had to be imported at a great expense from the Chittagong District.

It would, I think, have been wise had we recognized and modified this hill institution, not as slavery, but as a labour contract, which could be formally entered into and registered. So much money lent to be repaid by a certain period of voluntary labour, or so much cash; but above all, measures should have been taken to make the language of the Courts identical with the vernacular of the people.

There is another, a detestable and actual slavery in these hills, which formerly existed among our own tributary tribes, but is now only carried on by the independent tribes beyond our jurisdiction. This is the captivity to the bow and spear:—men and women taken prisoners by force in war, and sold like cattle from master to master. The origin of this custom, if not indeed the origin of the chronic state of warfare in which all hill people seem to live, was the want of women.

Among all hill people the woman is the hardest worker, the chief toiler[4]; and naturally enough their constant and incessant labour in all weathers kills the women of a tribe, or renders them more liable to the insidious attacks of disease. Hence, among some tribes, as the Todas of the Neilgherries for instance, we find the strange custom of polyandry prevailing; but among the tribes here a simpler course was adopted—the law of the strongest:

> "The good old rule, the simple plan,
> That he shall take who has the power,
> And he shall keep who can."

Those who had few women went with arms in their hands, and took what they wanted from a weaker community. Another custom, which too often served as a cloak for the obtaining of slaves, was that of demanding "goung hpo," a usage answering to the

[4] Among the Khyoungtha only, the women are placed on an equal footing with the men of the tribe in respect to work. The Shendoo tribe are also said to grant great privileges to their women; but our information as to this tribe is not very reliable.

"wehrgeld," or composition for the homicide of a relative, which occupies so large a place in the ancient jurisprudence of the Germans. This is the cause or pretext of almost every raid that is committed. It is the enforcement of demands, either of claims made by a strong village on a weak one for "ata" (black mail), or the price of the head (Arracanese "goung," a head, and "hpo," price) of some diseased member of the stronger community. It is the practice among them, on the death of any member of the village, to saddle it upon some village which he may lately have visited, and to demand a certain price for his life.

THE KHYOUNGTHA.

The Khyoungtha are subdivided into clans, mostly taking their names from the different streams on which they live.

They all dwell in village communities having a Roaja, or village head, through whom they pay revenue. The villages to the south of the Kurnafoolee River are subject to a Chief, called the Bohmong (from the Arracanese "boh," a head, and "mong," leader), whose residence is at Bundrabun, on the Sungoo River, while those to the north of the Kurnafoolee acknowledge the supremacy of the Mong Rajah[5]. The tribute paid to these Chiefs is from four to eight rupees yearly for each family. Unmarried men, priests, widows, widowers, and men who do not cultivate but live by the chase of wild beasts, are exempted from paying tribute. In addition to the money payment, each adult is liable to work for three days in each year, without pay, at the Chief's bidding. An offering of the first fruits of rice and cotton of every man's field is also made to the Chief. The position of Roaja, or village head, is more an honourable than a profitable one: he is chosen by the villagers, and appointed by the Chief, to whom he must present a "nuzzer" on his nomination being ratified. The office, generally speaking, descends from father to son. The Roaja decides all petty cases and disputes that may occur

[5] The Chukma tribe and their Chief will be noticed subsequently.

in the village, and for so doing he receives certain fees from both parties, according to custom and the importance of the case. In some instances he receives from the Chief a percentage on the yearly revenue collections.

Colonel Sir A. Phayre, in his account of Arracan (Journal Asiatic Society of Bengal, No. 117 of 1841) says that the Khyoungtha and Rakhoingtha, or Arracanese, are of the same race. Like the Burmans, their national name is Myamma, or, as it is pronounced in these hills, Murma. Rakhoingtha signifies an inhabitant of the Rakhoing country, while Khyoungtha means those who inhabit the banks of mountain streams, and support themselves by hill cultivation.

To the Bengallees of the plains the Khyoungtha is known by the name of Hill Mugh, but this is entirely a misnomer. Colonel Sir A. Phayre rightly states that this name exclusively belongs to a class of people residing in the Chittagong District, called Rajbunsees, or Mughs, who are the offspring of Bengallee women by Burmans when the latter possessed

Chittagong. They are well known in Calcutta as Mugh cooks, and are doubtless worthy people in their way, but are far removed in regard to manliness, uprightness, and all that we think noble, from the Khyoungtha of the hills. The Khyoungtha, like the Burmese, are Buddhists, and believe in the doctrine of metempsychosis, or the transmigration of souls. Each successive life is as it were a furnace by which the soul is refined, and so rises, step by step, to perfection, until eventually the state of "Nieban" is attained. I have heard stories of men who, in dying, thought they were sure of attaining this culminating point of perfection, and who are said to have expired with a very similar phrase in their mouths to that recorded of one of the Cæsars on his deathbed—"Ut puto Deus fio." This state of existence has in general been represented to mean merely annihilation, but this is not the case; such at least is not the idea that Buddhists attach to it. Crawford in his "Ava," Vol. II., Appendix, No. II., page 140, says that this misconception has thrown an unmerited share of obloquy on the worship of Buddha. Dr. Buchanan remarks that the term has been incorrectly translated (As. Researches, Vol. VI., p. 189); and Coleridge defined it correctly in his Essay on the Philosophy of Indian Sectaries (R. A. S. Trans., Vol. I., p. 566). We say that God is Heaven, and the Buddhists also believe that in "Nieban" they are incorporated with God, absorbed in, and partaking of, the perfection and ecstatic calm surrounding and emanating from the great central power of the universe.

Before their conversion to Buddhism, they probably performed the same simple natural religious rites which we see to this day among the wilder hill tribes, that is, offerings of rice, fruit and flowers, to the spirits of hill and river. This custom, indeed, although very unorthodox, is followed by most of the Khyoungtha at the present time. There is no such thing as caste among them; all are equal. It is in the power of any one who feels a vocation for it, to devote himself to

H

the service of God, and become a "Raheyn." He will then leave father, mother, wife, and children; and, dependent for clothes and daily bread upon his fellow-countrymen, he will pass his time in prayer, the education of the young, and the ministration of such ceremonies as funerals, fasts, &c., in which his fellow-men require the sanction and assistance of a minister of religion. Neither is it "once a priest, always a priest;" for should he find out that he has mistaken his vocation, he can leave it, and again become a member of the laity, living, loving, and marrying as they do.

The ceremonies of Buddhistic worship are simple and few: the presence of a priest is not indispensably necessary; prayers are made and offerings of flowers, food, &c., are placed before the shrine of their great apostle Gaudama by the people themselves. In many villages, indeed, there is no priest; and as the priesthood are a peripatetic fraternity, this does not much matter. The priest in fact is not so much a minister of religion, as a recipient of alms,—a holy man who has given up this world and its pleasures, and devoted himself to God. Hence it is, I think, that the priesthood in Burmah have never been the grasping and ambitious body that they have been at one time or another in all other countries in the world; hence, also, that in the struggle between Buddhism and Brahmanism, the former, the pure and self-denying faith speedily fell before the popularity-seeking religion of the Hindoo priest. Buddhism is a levelling faith; in matters relating to man and his soul it admits of no distinctions; there is no royal road to Paradise; the only superiority of man over man is gained by virtue and good deeds. No one can go among a people professing the Buddhist faith without seeing their superiority in manliness, truth, self-denial, and all the sterner, nobler class of moral excellences. These characteristics have naturally operated strongly in raising the social status of the weaker sex; and among our hill Buddhists, women are respected, and occupy an honourable position. They enjoy great freedom of action, and are unmistakably a power among the people. They, as well as the other sex, can work out their own salvation and attain "Nieban." In many parts of the hills may be seen aged women, who in the close of their life have devoted themselves to God's service; they occupy separate houses, however, and do not live in the "khiongs," or temples.

In each village is seen the "khiong," or house of religion. It is a bamboo structure raised some six feet from the ground, generally built under the shade of some trees, with a clear space in front, where the young men disport themselves in the evening. Inside, on a small raised platform of bamboo, stands an image of Gaudama, the last Boodh, made either of wood gilt over, or of alabaster. The image is generally in a sitting posture, with the pagoda-shaped head-dress indicative of supreme power. Before it are placed offerings of flowers and rice, which are brought fresh every morning by the girls of the village, who, at the same time, bring, in covered trays, the daily food of any priest or wayfarer who may be resting there. Around the walls of the "Khiong" are hung the black boards on which the village youngsters learn to read and write. By the side of the image of Boodh generally hangs a small stand of bells, and morning and evening the villagers in twos and threes will ascend the small log of wood, cut into steps, by which the "khiong" is approached, remove their turbans, and on hands and knees reverently salute the semblance of their revered teacher, first ringing the bells to let him know that they are there. Each one prays for himself, save that now and again a father may be seen leading his young son by the hand and teaching him how to pray. The "khiong" is the great resort of all the bachelors of the village; it is there that all the talk and gossip goes on. At evening time, when the sun westers, and it grows cool, they assemble at the "khiong;" the lads and lasses play at "konyon" on the clear space below, while the elders sit above and peacefully chat, smoking their cigars.

The game of "konyon" is played universally by all the hill tribes; it is very popular, and causes considerable excitement and emulation among the players. The "konyon," from whence the game derives its name, is the seed of a creeper, in colour and smoothness like our English horse-chestnut; it is about an inch and a half in diameter, and half an inch thick, in shape circular and flattish, with a small level spot at the base of the seed on which it is placed edgewise for the players to pitch at. Each player has his own "konyon;" the great art is to nick your opponent and knock his seed over. The "konyon" is propelled by the middle finger of the right hand, which serves as a sort of spring pulled back by the left. The side gaining most nicks wins.

Every year at the "khiong," just before the commencement of the jooming season, the ceremony of "shiang pruhpo" occurs. This is a religious rite, approaching closely in significance to our "confirmation." The young boys of the village, on attaining the age of eight or nine years, are clothed in the yellow garments of the priesthood, have their heads shaved, and at the "khiong" go through a ceremony which seems to be on their part a kind of assumption of religious duties. They sit all in a circle before the priest; before each one is an offering according to the means of his parents, of rice or cloth, and before each burns a little lamp, which is kept trimmed and bright during the ceremony by the sponsor, or nearest male relative of each, who sits behind; each of the acolytes reverently joins his hands, bows his head, and makes the responses after the presiding priest. After the ceremony they remain in the "khiong" dressing and living as priests for seven days, during which time they must eat simply, and indulge in no sports or vain pastimes. Women do not participate in this rite, but it is common for a man to perform it two or three times during his life. Is any one dear to him sick, or has he escaped from any danger, he performs the "shiang" as a kind of acknowledgment of God's mercy, or a supplication for forbearance. In the Hill Tracts, besides the small "khiongs" (temporary structures built of bamboo), which are found in every village, there are two temples sacred to Buddha, to which the hill people resort in large numbers at the time of their festival in May. One temple is situated at Bundrabun, the residence of the Bohmong, and the other in the Chittagong District, Thannah Raojan, close to the border of the Hill Tracts. This latter temple is known by the name of Mahamunnee. This would appear to be a name brought from Arracan, for Colonel Phayre, in his account of Arracan (B. Asiatic Society's Journal, No. 1451, 18844), says that "King Tsanda-thoo-vee-ya built the Mahamunnee temple in Arracan in honour of a visit of the Boodh Gaudama. I have frequently been present at these religious gatherings, and the scene is a strange one. An account of a visit paid by me last year to a religious festival at the Mahamunnee temple may not perhaps be out of place here.

On arriving at the spot, the first thing that attracted my attention was the temple. It was square in shape, standing in the centre of a small bricked court, the outer wall of which, however, was not more than five feet high, so that one could look over it. I ascertained that there was no objection to my entering the temple, and then proceeded to view the interior. The centre was occupied by an enormous sitting figure of Gaudama, the last Boodh, of about 50 feet in height, painted and gilt. This was the inner shrine, and round it ran a square vaulted corridor, on all four sides, about 12 feet broad and perhaps 150 feet square. On entering this outer corridor, which, being but scantily furnished with windows, was in comparative darkness, I saw before me a shaven-headed yellow-robed priest, sitting on the ground, surrounded by a crouching circle of devotees. The bowed heads of the postulants were shaven, and through their hands, from man to man, ran a white thread, the two ends of which were held by the priest, who, with an unmoved aspect, undisturbed by my entrance, was monotonously reciting a prayer or invocation, which was repeated in a broken jumble by the persons before and around him. At his feet was a small heap of money, doubtless the offerings of the neophytes; and before each man was a vessel of water containing fresh green leaves. The devotees were males of all ages: some boys of eight to ten, some adults, and one old man. I found that this ceremony was a dedication of themselves to the service of Gaudama, involving a course of fasting and abstinence from all secular amusements and thoughts for a short period, generally of nine days, answering, I fancy, to the French 'neuvaine.' After they had been duly consecrated, they assumed the yellow garments of the priesthood, to be doffed, however, at the expiration of their period of retirement. The ceremony is, I believe, by no means a penitential one; but it is supposed that an occasional exercise of self-discipline is pleasing to the deity, and likely to bring good fortune, especially when, as at present, it is performed at the commencement of the year. The place of the gathering lay just at the junction of the plains and hills; and from both directions, as the day drew on, and the shadows began to lengthen, characteristic groups began to make their appearance. From the plains came the well-known greasy bunniah in his chronic condition of perspiration; the plausible cloth-merchant (what native can adjust a turban like him?); the black and sinewy coppersmith; and the general storekeeper: this latter being generally a Mussulman of middle age and debauched appearance. These all began to establish themselves in temporary bamboo sheds or shanties, which formed lines converging on the shrine as a centre. Much more pleasant (to my eyes at least) were the different bands of hill people, who might be seen coming in, party after party, from the direction where in the distance rose the wooded hills, blue against the horizon. Their parties were always village communities, numbering from eight to ten up to thirty individuals. First would be seen the drummer, who advanced with the proud consciousness of leadership to a spirited accompaniment on the tom-tom. Next came the village head man, or Roaja, dressed in clean, white, home-spun garments, with his scarlet-bordered cloth wound round his shoulders, toga fashion. After him would come his wife, middle-aged, but still of a comely presence. She would generally have a flower in her hair, and carry in one hand an earthen-bowled pipe with silver stem. Following her, one by one, would troop in the maidens, dressed very becomingly, with a white turban loosely bound round their heads, their faces (very pretty ones in some cases) exposed, bearing a merry, frank expression, while from their luxuriant black hair would peep a flower, a lemon-coloured orchid, or some bright jungle creeper-blossom. They wore a dark-blue skirt of home-spun cloth with a scarlet border. Round their bosoms was wound a soft, white cloth, barred with chocolate-coloured stripes; and in case the girls were of wealthy family, they would have a silver chain round their necks, or wear perhaps a skirt of purple silk instead of the dark-blue home-spun. Sometimes a young lady would be seen saucily puffing a roll of tobacco, cigar fashion, while she turned to talk, over her shoulder, to some tall, strapping young villager, her betrothed perhaps, who would walk quietly in the rear, carrying on his back, slung over his forehead, in hill fashion, the long basket, or 'tooroong,' containing the supplies of his party. There were generally more women than men in the parties, and some of them had even brought with them their little ones to share in the good luck which was to accrue to the pilgrims. Night closed in, and still party after party thronged to the place in close succession. As each village company arrived they defiled before the temple, not entering however, but each one making a salute with both hands joined as they passed, and then proceeding to take up their quarters under the trees around. There they lit fires; the women began to cook; and the social pipe was passed from hand to hand. As I went to sleep that night, the gathering hum of many voices and of laughter was borne to my ears on the night-wind, mingled with the melody of the hill 'basuli,' or clarionet, and interspersed with the wild hill cry, which is like a quadruplicated Australian 'Cooey.' The sound of the basuli strangely reminded me of the Swiss Ranz des Vaches.

"The next morning the festa was in full swing. The temple was surrounded by a fringe of saffron-robed, shaven-headed priests, or 'Shiang Phras,' as they are called, sitting in dull-eyed abstraction, each one under the shade of his own enormous red umbrella. Some of them were telling their beads; others, spectacles on nose, were gravely mumbling forth sacred readings from bundles of strange Pali-covered palm leaves; here and there I noticed a repetition of the swearing-in ceremony of the night before. The temple itself was crammed with devotees, male and female, all hill people, every one, not a Bengallee among them. Their devotion, which was energetic, consisted apparently in walking round and round the outer corridor surrounding the image, in pairs of man and maid, or occasionally in male fours. Whenever these male fours were organized squalls were imminent, for the blithe young bachelors, each with a flower behind his left ear, a basuli in his hand, and a roll of tobacco in his mouth, would jauntily parade round the sacred building, stretching forth a lawless arm towards any female they might pass, now disarranging the turban of some buxom matron, again snatching a kiss from some little maiden shrinking under the wing of her father or brother; and naturally these little familiarities would occasionally produce a row. Immediately, however, any such disagreement seemed impending, both parties would be seized and promptly bundled out of the temple, while the women would be surrounded, and carried round and round the corridor, in the midst of a knot of laughing, teasing lads. The majority of the people at the fair were young; hardly a single old man or woman, indeed, could be seen.

"Outside, in the bazaar, the throng was equally close. Here were shops whose whole stock-in-trade consisted of long strings of small, yellow candles and heaps of crackers; there was a vendor, who dealt, to all appearance, exclusively in red threads, strings of coloured beads, and cheap fiddles. The sweetmeat shops came out in magnificent style, and here one would often see some well-looking lad treating his sweetheart to cakes, or loitering, hand in hand with her, to the next stall, where in rich and dazzling profusion were displayed bright-yellow silk handkerchiefs, with a flaring red pattern, and fine, white muslins, such as could not be made at home in the villages. One enterprising speculator had brought hither a peep-show, evidently the first thing of the sort that had ever been seen in the country, if one might judge by the crowds of men and women round it, all eager to see, at one pice per peep, the marvels of Delhi, Calcutta, &c., contained within the magic-box. The shops of the coppersmiths glistened with all sorts of shining and quaintly shaped vessels, while above all the din and clamour was heard the never-ceasing, wailing melody of the hill basuli. This music has a strange and characteristic effect on the hill people. I have seen women weep at the sound, and no hill man would dream of entering upon a courtship without the aid of his basuli. At night the scene was rendered, if possible, more picturesque by the lighting up of innumerable small candles, of which every one carried one, and some enthusiastic worshippers as many as four. Crackers also added to the life of the scene, and to fasten one to a woman's dress seemed to be thought as great fun here as it would have been at an English fair.

"Round and round went the stream of pilgrims in the outer corridor, singing as they went in strophe and anti-strophe of male and female voices. Not for a single hour, day or night, was there, as far as I could ascertain, any intermission to this constant circling; as some became tired, their places were supplied by others, and this lasted for three days. On the day on which the fair terminated, some six or eight long bamboos, with pendant white flags of coarse cotton cloth, ornamented with a fringe of split bamboo, were erected with great ceremony in front of the temple. I saw one village community also of about thirty souls, who, before leaving, underwent a blessing from one of the priests. The ceremony was in this wise:—A small hole was dug in the ground, and in it some silver and copper coins were placed, and water poured over them; over this was erected a small tripod of split bamboo, which was crowned with fresh, green leaves, and round this again was wound the mystic white thread, which, extending thence, passed through the hands of all the circle, who received it kneeling, passing finally into the hands of the Shiang Phra. In the centre knelt the village headman and his wife, both elderly and honest-looking. Mumble-mumble went the venerable priest, dragging his beads slowly through his fingers, and 'make haste, father,' cried a pretty, coquettish-looking little wench in the circle, 'the rice is getting cold;' for which piece of ill-timed levity she was soundly rated by the house-mother at the conclusion of the ceremony. An hour after that the whole grove was empty, and all the gay crowd of honest, simple people had disappeared as quickly as they had come; nothing was to be seen but a stray shopkeeper here and there, packing his goods, or reckoning his profits."

The dress of the Khyoungtha is simple. The men wear a "dhoyak," or cloth of soft, home-spun cotton, round the middle, reaching from the hips to below the knee. In persons of rank the "dhoyak" is longer, reaching almost to the ground, and is generally made of silk or fine muslin; to this is added a "ranjee," or short jacket with sleeves, tying or buttoning at the throat. All males wear the "goungboung," or turban, which, however, is wound round the head in the manner different to that of the natives of Hindoostan. As a rule, no shoes are worn. The women generally do not wear a turban, but on feast or festival days they bind a bright-coloured kerchief loosely round the hair. Around the bosom is wound a cloth about a span wide, the arms and neck being exposed. They wear also a "tabween" (called "tamuin" in Burmese), or petticoat of cotton or silk. It has no tie or fastening, but is brought round the waist with the edges twisted in and kept on by the swell of the hips. It is open in front, and single, so that in walking the right leg and part of the thigh are exposed. The men often tattoo their arms and legs with blue figures of dragons and other arabesques; it is usual also to tattoo the name of God on the shoulder. This custom of tattooing originated, they say, in ancient times among the people of Sandoway in Arracan, as well as the somewhat free dress of the women. A certain queen noticed with regret that the men of the nation were losing their love for the society of the women, and were resorting to vile and abominable practices, from which the worst possible results might be expected. She therefore prevailed upon her husband to promulgate a rigorous order, prescribing the form of petticoat to be worn by all women in future, and directing that the males should be tattooed in order that, by thus disfiguring the males, and adding piquancy to the beauty of the women, the former might once more return to the feet of their wives.

This custom, however, as regards women's dress, is probably of very ancient origin, for it is recorded in Plutarch's Lives, in his comparison between Numa and Lycurgus, with reference to the Spartan women, that "the skirts of the habit which the virgins wore were not sewed to the bottom, but opened at the side, as they walked, and discovered the thigh."

Men and women both among the Khyoungtha are passionately fond of flowers; it is the offering of women to the gods, of men to their mistresses. The young maidens wear constantly in their hair the graceful white or orange-coloured blossom of the numerous orchids with which the forest abounds; and a young man will rise long before dawn and climb the loftiest hills and trees to win his sweetheart's smile, by bringing her a flower that others do not possess. The males generally stick a bunch of flowers or sweet-smelling herbs into the turban, or through the lobe of the ear, which is generally pierced with a large hole, which serves also as a receptacle for a spare cheroot.

Of ornaments, both sexes alike wear pendant earrings and bracelets of silver or gold. The women wear in addition large truncated hollow cones of silver stuck through the lobe of the ear; these are used as flower-holders. Beads of coral for the neck are also much prized as a female ornament.

Their mode of kissing is strange: instead of pressing lip to lip, they apply the mouth and nose to the cheek, and give a strong inhalation. In their language they do not say, "Give me a kiss;" but they say, "Smell me."

In the village communities, even as the

adults have a recognized village head, so also is there a head boy appointed to control the boys of the village. This custom seems to prevail among all hill people. Mr. Hunter, in his "Annals of Rural Bengal" (page 217), records that a similar arrangement prevails among the Sonthals. This head of the juvenile community is called the "goung." I shall give here, as illustration of their village customs, a recital which I heard told at the camp fire one night in the jungles, by one of our policemen of the Palaingtsa clan. He said, "I was formerly goung over the unmarried lads of Hmraphroo village; this was when I was about seventeen years old. At night, all who were unmarried, and weaned from their mothers, used to sleep in the 'khiong.' One night Ougjyn, and Reyphaw, and Chaindra, came to me and got leave to go and sleep with their sweethearts. The girls were named Aduhbyn, Hlapyn, and Aduhsheay. I remember their names quite well; they are married now, and two of them have children. Our lads went by stealth, of course: if the parents had known it there would have been a row. Next day a little girl told me that Pynhla, another of our lads, who had not got leave to sleep out, had passed the night with her sister. This was quite contrary to rule, and it was therefore determined to punish him. Next day we all went to the Roaja's joom to help to build his house, and in the evening, when we returned, we made a big fire on the bank of the stream that runs through the village; and I sent and called Pynhla, but he was afraid, and would not come; he stayed in his father's house, and said he had fever. I knew this was only an excuse; so I sent three lads to bring him forcibly, and they went and brought him, although his mother abused them much; but the father and mother could not hurt them, as they were acting by the 'goung's' order. When he came, I called upon him to say why he had slept away from the 'khiong' without leave. At first he denied all about it, and then I brought forward the little girl, and he asked her, 'How did you know it was

I? it was dark;' and she said, 'The moon shone on your face in the early morning when you opened the door to go away.' When he heard this he saw there was no escape, and he fell at my feet and asked forgiveness; but I fined him three rupees on the spot for the sake of discipline." In Colonel Dalton's paper on the Coles of Chota Nagpore, he speaks of their being in each village of the Oraoon tribe a bachelors' hall where all the young unmarried men sleep at night. He mentions also that the elder lads are placed in authority over the younger. In front of the bachelors' hall a cleared space is kept for games and dancing. It is curious to observe how similar are the customs prevailing among the tribes here.

According to European ideas, the standard of morality among the Khyoungtha is low. It is not thought a crying sin for a maiden to yield to the solicitations of her lover before marriage; indeed, a girl generally has two or three sweethearts before settling down to a wedded life. The intercourse between the sexes before marriage is almost entirely unrestricted, although the Khyoungtha in this respect are rather stricter than the other and wilder tribes. After marriage, however, chastity is the rule, and one seldom hears of such a thing as an unfaithful wife; and this is not improbable, as marriages in the hills are unions of inclination, and not of interest. Some girls there are who marry their first love, but the proverbial inconstancy of man extends even to these hills, and the lover but too often only gathers the flower in order to throw it away. Girls marry at the age of about sixteen, and a young man generally begins to think of taking a wife before he reaches the age of nineteen years. The women sometimes do not think it beneath them to make advances in a modest way. One of our police constables came to me one day to ask for leave of absence for a week. I asked him why. He said, "A young maiden of such a village has sent me flowers and birnee rice twice as a token, and if I wait any longer, they will say I am no man."

Pawn and betel are universally eaten by the Khyoungtha, and they are not unfrequently used as a means wherewith to make amatory propositions. Thus a leaf of pawn with betel and sweet spices inside, accompanied by a certain flower, means, "I love you." If much spice is put inside the leaf, and one corner turned in a peculiar way, it signifies, "Come." The leaf being touched with turmeric means, "I cannot come." A small piece of charcoal inside the leaf is, "Go, I have done with you." Love-songs have they in plenty, called "kapya." The great place for singing this kind of song is when working in the jooms at the time of harvest. At this time the lads and lasses work in a crowd together. Then some youth will take up the word thus:—

The hills stretch in long ranges marshaued by God.
The kramoo flower and dymbyn,
Oh, maidens, do not sow.
The hills stretch in long ranges, God driven;
The cockscomb (kramoo) and the dyn flowers
Even should you sow,
Maidens, do not wear them;
The kramo and dym flowers, if worn,
As they fade, a maiden's heart withers away.

As he finishes, the whole party break into the "hoia," or hill call; and far away down the mountain, or from another ridge, the call will be repeated and taken up by hill man after hill man, till it dies away in the distance. Then there will be a little silence among the girls, and they will say, "Do you answer him, Pynchynda?" "No, I cannot sing: I am hoarse to-day, I have not got my voice, and he is in voice like a koel-bird;" and jest and counter-jest will be bandied among them, until some young girl lifts up her voice and replies:—

A dweller in the mountain is the bumble bee;
He lives in a dead bamboo,
On the hill side.

Then a young man will sing again thus:—

From afar off I see the waters of the Kynsa,
White in the valley.
What good have I from gazing on it,
Some other will bathe therein.

[All give the "hoia."]

From afar off gazing, I see a maiden;
White and fair is she.
What good have I from looking on her,
Some more fortunate one will obtain her love.

[Grand "hoia."]

Or this:—

A flock of birds;
One bird only, on a high tree sitting
All alone.
Of men, a crowd:
One man only, without a companion,
Has no happiness.

There are hundreds of these songs. The above, which are almost literal translations, will serve as examples.

The marriage ceremony of the Khyoungtha is distinctive and uncommon. On a young man attaining a marriageable age, that is, about seventeen or eighteen, his parents look about for some young girl who would be a good wife to him, unless, as is more often the case, he has fixed upon a partner for himself. Having determined upon a suitable match, a male relative of the family is sent off to the girl's parents to arrange matters. On arriving at their village, he proceeds to the house; and before going up the house-ladder, he gives the usual salutation, with both hands joined and raised to the forehead. "*Ogatsa*," he says, "a boat has come to your landing-place; will you bind it or loose it?" A favourable response is given, and he then goes up into the house. On seating himself, he asks, "Are the supports of the house firm?" If the answer is, "They are firm," it is favourable, and matters may then be more fully entered into. The affair is taken into consideration, and he returns to his own village to report good progress to the bridegroom's parents, and to request them to fix a day for taking the omens. On the appointed day the parents meet, the young people being supposed to know nothing of all this. A fowl is killed by the fathers, its tongue taken out, and, according to certain marks thereon, the matter is pronounced good or bad. The bridegroom's parents sleep for the night at the house of the intended bride, and all parties look anxiously for dreams by which to foretell the happiness or the reverse of the union. On going away, should every thing be propitious, their intended daughter kneels at their feet for a blessing, and they present her with a new petticoat and a silver ring. Learned persons are then called in, who, by consulting the stars, and casting the nativity of the parties, determine a favourable day and hour when the ceremony shall be undertaken. Meantime the parents on both sides prepare pigs and spirits, rice and spices, unlimited, for the marriage feast. They also send round to all their kith and kin a fowl and a letter giving notice of the intended marriage; in some places a pice or copper coin is substituted for the fowl. On the auspicious day, and at the hour appointed, the bridegroom and all his relatives set out for the bride's house, dressed in the gayest colours, both men and women, with drums beating before them. On arriving at the entrance of the village, the female relatives of the bride bar the approach with a bamboo. Across this barrier the bridegroom has to drink a loving cup of fraternity, generally spirits. Should the females on the bride's side muster strong, the road will probably be barred five or six times before the entry into the village is fairly made. The bridegroom, however, does not drink all that is given him;

but after taking the liquor in his mouth, he is allowed to eject it again upon the ground.

In the village, on some open turfy spot, a number of bamboo booths have been erected, adorned with flowers and green boughs, and filled with materials for feasting. Here also sit an opposition party of drummers, and mighty is the row as the bridegroom's party defiles on to this spot. A separate and specially beautified booth has been erected for the young lover and his parents, and here they sit in state and receive visits from all the village. The bride in like manner, surrounded by her near relatives, sits in her father's house. The boys of the village, irrepressible as is the wont of that species, make raids upon both parties, for the purpose of chaffing and getting alternate feasts of comestibles. They also organize an amateur band of music, and serenade the bride towards evening with fiddles and flutes. Of course, all the girls of the village are congregated at the bride's father's house, and, as license and riot are the order of the day, the fun here grows fast and furious. Towards nightfall the bridegroom ascends to his bride's house amid a tempest of cheers and a hailstorm of drums. After this outburst a temporary lull ensues, to permit of the ceremony being performed. The bride is brought forth from an inner chamber in the arms of the women. On the floor of the house are placed water in jars, rice, and mango leaves. Round these a new-spun cotton-thread is wound and carried again round the two contracting parties as they stand opposite to each other. The "poongyee," or priest, now comes forward; he recites some prayers in a language that is not understood even by himself (probably Pali), and then taking cooked rice, a handful in each hand, he crosses and re-crosses his arms, giving seven alternate mouthfuls to the bride and bridegroom; after this he takes their hands and crooks the little finger of the bridegroom's right hand into the little finger of the bride's left. The ceremony is then concluded by more unintelligible mutterings. The bridegroom now takes the bride by the hand, and together they make the circuit of the room, saluting lowly the elder relatives of both families. They then sit down, the bride to the left of her husband, and their clothes are tied together. The wedding guests then come forward and place at their feet, each according to his or her means, some presents of clothes or household furniture.

After this, a saturnalia ensues, of dancing, drinking, fighting, and love-making. The bride and bridegroom are expected to sit up all night. I should add that the happy man does not consummate his marriage until he and his wife (sleeping apart) have for seven days eaten together seven times a day. After marriage a younger brother is allowed to touch the hand, to speak and laugh with his elder brother's wife; but it is thought improper for an elder even to look at the wife of his younger brother. This is a custom more or less among all hill tribes; it is found carried to even a preposterous extent among the Sonthals. In Man's account of Sonthalia (p. 100), in describing a Sonthal wedding, he says, "I remarked with surprise the alarming familiarities displayed by the youthful brother of the bridegroom to the bride, and was told that it was the custom for the younger brother, if unmarried, to take the face of his elder brother's bride (as Lady Duff Gordon would say)."

From marriage to death is no very long stride. The moment we begin to live, we begin to die. Marriage is generally the half-way house between the womb of our mother and the bosom of Terra Mater.

When a person has died, his relatives assemble. Some one of them sits down and commences to beat the funeral roll on the drum; the women weep and cry; and the men busy themselves, some in performing the last offices to the corpse, of washing, dressing, &c., while others go off to the woods and bring wood for the funeral pile, and bamboos, with which to construct the bier. About twenty-four hours generally elapse from the time of death to that of cremation. In bearing the corpse from the house to the burning ground, if the deceased were a man of wealth or influence, the body may be borne on a wheeled car; all women also have this privilege; the plebs, however, are simply carried to the funeral pile on the shoulders of their relatives. The procession is after this fashion:— First come the priests, if there are any in the vicinity to attend; they march gravely at the head of the party, bearing on their shoulders their curved palm-leaf fans, clad in their ordinary saffron-coloured robes, and attended by their disciples. Next come relatives of the deceased, two and two, bearing food, clothes, &c., which have been offered as alms to the priests on behalf of the departed. Next is borne the bier carried on bamboos by six men and accompanied by as many drums as can be procured. Behind the coffin come the male relatives; and lastly, the procession is closed by the women of the village, clad in their best. The funeral pile is composed of four layers of wood for a woman, three for a man. The body is placed on the pile; the leading priest takes an end of the dead man's turban, and, holding it, repeats some passages of the law, four of the deceased's male relatives standing meanwhile at the four corners of the pile, and sprinkling a few drops of water thereon. The nearest blood relative, male or female, of the dead man then fires the pile. When the fire is extinguished, the ashes are scrupulously collected together and buried over the spot: a small conical mound of earth is heaped up, and a very long bamboo pole, with an equally lengthy flag, is erected over the grave. On returning from the place, all parties bathe themselves. If it is the master of the house who has died, the ladder leading up to the house is thrown down, and they must effect an entrance by cutting a hole in the back wall and so creeping up. The relatives eat and drink, and each contributes according to his means to defray the expenses incurred. After seven days the priests re-assemble at the house to read prayers for the dead.

The Khyoungtha have one fault, that although cleanly in their other habits, they allow their hair to become very filthy. Both sexes allow their hair to grow long, and seldom wash it; the consequences may therefore be better imagined than described. The women wear their hair, which is long, black, and rather coarse, twisted into a coil at the back of the head, and fastened by a silver bodkin, attached to which is a chain of the same metal, which is wound twice round the knot of hair at the back. The use of false hair among both men and women is universal; it is plaited in at the back to make the knot look bigger. The sale of false hair is carried on at every market attended by hill people throughout the district. The men for the most part tie their hair in a knot at the back. In this they differ from both the Rakoingtha and the Burmese, who wear the hair in a more manly way, coiled and knotted on the top of the head over the temple. With regard to this custom, the Bohmong Chief related to me the following tradition:—

"In former times, when the Moghuls were Rajahs in Chittagong, and Arracan was an independent monarchy, my ancestors lived on the Koladan River in Arracan. Now, the King of Burmah was very jealous of the King of Arracan, and wished to take his kingdom from him. So he called all his wise men together, and took counsel, saying, 'Who will go to the King of Arracan, and by magic arts bring him low? Whoever will do this, I will advance him to great honour, and make him equal to myself.' On this, one wise man stepped forth and said, 'I will do this thing.' So this wise man left all his family in Burmah, but took with him a woman of low character to represent his wife, so that the King of Arracan might have faith in him; and he came to Arracan, and represented to the King that he was a fugitive from before the King of Burmah, that he was well acquainted with magical arts, but that because he would not transform the houses of the capital into pure gold, therefore the King of Burmah sought his life. He could have turned all the houses into gold if he had been so minded, said the narrator. So the King of Arracan took him into favour, and assigned him a house and provision from the royal table; and daily he grew and increased in the King's favour. So when the King listened much to his words, he began to flatter him, saying that, 'If you will listen to me I can make your empire increase indefinitely, and you will be able to subdue both the Burmans and Moghuls, and all foreign countries.' 'How will you enable me to do this?' said the King. The wise man replied, 'Your city is built without magic; I must first see to that, for unless you inhabit a prosperous and a safe abode you cannot expect to succeed in great enterprizes.' So the King gave orders that he should do what he would, and that no one should interfere with him; and the wise man levelled all the walls of the royal city and laid it open to attack; and he buried at the four corners a charm by which the inhabitants became faint-hearted. Next, he told the King, 'You must not bind your hair in a knot on the forehead, as your forefathers have done, but must tie it in a coil behind, as the women do—you and all your people.' So the King obeyed him, and ordered that all his subjects should do the like. This wise man also caused the shape of the spoon used in Arracan to be altered, and filed down the King's teeth. When he had reduced the whole country to a condition of woman's weakness, he pretended to be ill, and shutting himself up in his house, gave orders that he should not be disturbed while he was performing the last charm necessary to render the King invincible; and he put unhusked rice in a pot, over his extinguished fire, and sprinkled it with water till it began to sprout, and so at night he fled away. After some time the King became uneasy at his adviser's long seclusion, and he began to search, saying, 'Where is my guide and my teacher?' Then the guards searched the house of the wise man and found it empty, and the grain sprouting in the pot; so they went and told the King that the wise man must have been carried away many days ago, and that it was an evil demon in his shape that had latterly been seen, for that the rice in his pot had sprouted, and had evidently been there many months.

"Then came the King of Burmah with an army and took Arracan, and our King was killed, and my grandfather took the tribe and fled away into the Chittagong Hills; but to this day the charm of the wise man prevails, and we are not so brave as formerly, and wear our hair in a knot at the back of the head."

They are full of legends and stories, this people; their proverbs, also, are as the sands of the sea. Here are a few of them:—

1.	Aipaw peerey tummung go ma tcha.	Food refused when offered.
	Konye eyn tak paw, hrarey ma ra.	Search in seven houses, and you will not find.

This answers to our—

> "He that will not when he may,
> When he will he shall have nay."

2.	Khwee goung mha khee san yan.	Like a dog with a dirty head.
3.	Tchapo ma tai-kuey seerey.	The person not knowing how to eat will die.
	Toing po ma tai-kuey hruie rarey.	The person not knowing how to sit will get up.

4.	Wa la, wa kuoinrey, Tchang la, tchang phainrey.	The bamboo is bound by the bamboo, The elephant is caught by the elephant.

English synonyms :—

"Like goes to like;"
"Set a thief to catch a thief."

"The bamboo is bound by the bamboo," is an allusion to the way that the hill people build their houses; the whole house is built on bamboo poles, and these are bound together by the fibres of the bamboo twisted together into a sort of rope.

5.	Proa gyan ma heeguey. Shia lop ma ra. Lagyan ma heeguey. Akreelop ma ra.	From silence the tongue grows rusty; From long rest the legs grow disobedient.
6.	Seera seemey, nga amauk go ma koynguey wodong tcho hnewn.	If I must die, I must die; but do not touch my top-knot, as the peacock said.

This proverb reminds one of the picture by dear old John Leech, of the swell and the robber :—"Take all, take money, take life; but spare, oh! spare my collars."

In bathing, a Khyoungtha will never wet

his head, owing to the difficulty which he would afterwards experience in drying his thick, long hair. The consequence is, as I have said, that parasites therein are abundant. With reference to this point, I was one day taking a hill man to task for his dirtiness, and he told me the following story :—

"One day the head of the King of Arracan itched enormously; scratching was of no effect, and combing seemed rather to increase than allay the irritation. Now, at that time, lice were unknown to the people of Arracan; so he called to his wife, and said, 'My life, just fetch here your small tooth-comb, and see what is the matter with my head, as I have a feeling there as if a ground dog (the jackal) were burrowing for himself a nest in my brain.' So the Queen came and made him sit down; and searching vigorously, she found a parasitic insect, such as had never before been seen in that country. All the courtiers and the Queen's maids came up and inspected it, but no one was able to tell what it was.

The wise man and the astrologers were called, and they cast its nativity, and pronounced that this is not a born native of this country, as the stars give no information about it. Then the King was greatly puzzled, and again scratched his head in perplexity. At last he issued a proclamation throughout the kingdom, giving notice of this strange, new animal, and setting forth that whoever should come forward and disclose its name and origin should receive the hand of the princess, his daughter, in marriage. The insect, meanwhile, was carefully shut up in a golden box, and hung up at the head of the ladder leading to the palace, for all persons to inspect. Well, the King's proclamation went forth into all parts of the world, and there was at that time a 'rakus,' or ogre, who lived on the other side of the wall which surrounds the world, which God will throw down at the last day, and he heard this proclamation, and by virtue of his inner consciousness he at once became aware that this insect had come forth from the head of one Abulkhan, a merchant of the Kulas (Bengallees), who had come to the King's city to sell clothes, and who was at that time residing in the house of the chief minister in Arracan. So the 'rakus' took the form of a fair young man, and coming to the King's court, he said as much. On this the King sent and arrested the Kula merchant, and lo! it was so. Therefore, the merchant was cast into a den of serpents, and the King's youngest daughter, who was not a little beautiful, was espoused by the 'rakus.' After residing some time at the court, the 'rakus' became greatly afflicted with his cannibalistic longings, so much so that he was obliged to occupy a chamber alone for fear the temptation should prove too strong for him. At last, at his wife's solicitations, he went with her to his father-in-law, and having both performed obeisance, they requested permission to depart, which the King granted. A favourable day and hour were accordingly fixed upon by the astrologers, and the young couple set forth, accompanied by a guard of honour sent by the Queen-mother. Now the 'rakus' was very hungry; so he went a short day's journey, and there halting, informed his wife that he would take three of the guards with him and go out shooting. He no sooner, however, had entered the jungle, than he devoured the three men with much delight, and returning to the princess said that the three men who had accompanied him had returned to Arracan. This mode of acting he repeated every day, until, by the time they arrived at the borders of the great forest which separates the 'rakus' country from the rest of the world, all the guard had been made an end of. The princess, however, in her heart had not been without suspicions of her husband's mode of procedure; and the last time he had gone out shooting, she had followed him, and beheld the awful fate of the guard. When she saw this, she became greatly terrified, and flying back to the camp, she remained in prayer for her deliverance. Back came the 'rakus' eager for the discussion of the dainty bit which he had saved for his last mouthful;

and when the princess heard his hasty step, she prayed that 'if I have been chaste and good from my birth, let the lamp which I brought from my father's temple open and hide me from the 'rakus.' So the lamp opened, and she was hid just as her husband entered. The 'rakus' was greatly enraged at this, and he seized the lamp and hammered it, and cut it, but to no avail; so at last he threw it into a river that ran close by, and departed howling to his own country. The lamp was carried down by the next freshet of rain, and was found on the shore by a young prince, who took it up and kept it carefully in his chamber. When night came, the princess came out of the lamp and swept the room, cooked the prince's dinner, prepared pawn and betel, ate some herself, and touching the prince's dress with some of the red juice of the betel nut, she re-entered her lamp and was hidden. The prince was naturally much surprised in the morning to find his house in order without visible agency. This happened three nights in succession, and the third night the prince determined to lay awake; so he thrust a needle through his thumb in order that the pain might prevent his sleeping, and he reaped the reward of his watchfulness in surprising the princess while performing her self-imposed task. They were, of course, married, and lived happily ever afterwards."

It is by no means an uncommon thing for a young man to elope with his sweetheart, should the consent of the parents be difficult of attainment. I remember one young fellow, who, having made a runaway match of this description, came to me to sanction it; and his account of the proceeding was very curious, and threw much light on their village life. He said, "When I reached the village, it was nightfall; the village was empty, for the grain was now ripening, and every one was up in the jooms; so I stayed that night in the house of one Akra, in his joom. In the morning the house-mother woke me, saying, 'Hasten, get up; wash your face and make yourself smart, for to-day the girls of the village come here to reap our crop.' I looked down the hill, hearing the hoia (hill call) far away down the slope, and saw the girls coming, and the young men with them; so I hastened and tied my hair behind in a knot and put a silver bangle on my arm, and a gold bead hanging at my neck, and tied on my white turban sprucely, for these are the fashions of the Kowkdyntsa clan; and if one wants to get on with the people, one must conform to their customs. Then they arrived, and we all went out to cut the rice. After a time one young girl said to a companion, 'Pynchainda, sing to us;' so she sang, and afterwards she said, turning to me, 'Here is a young Palaingtsa come to see us. How bashful he is, and how young! When is he going to be married, I wonder!' and all the girls began making fun, until I was quite ashamed and could hardly cut the grain; the blood went all into my head. Then some one said, 'Sing to us, O brother;' so I sang, and they said, 'You sing well, sit you on that knoll, and sing to us while we work;' so I did so.

"At noon we had to eat, and the young girls came round me, and said, 'You have sung much to us, now you must eat:' but I replied, 'No, I am not hungry.' Then the house-mother said, 'What kind of maidens are you, to let a guest stand thus making excuses? Why, when I was a girl, we should have taken him by the hand and made him eat.' So five of the girls came and drew me forcibly to where the food was, and I said, 'If you will all eat out of the same dish with me, then I will eat;' so they agreed, and spread a mighty platter, and we all ate. They tried at first to feed me; but after a mouthful or two, for courtesy's sake, I said, 'No, at that rate I shall never be satisfied.'

"At night one of the young men said to me, 'Come, and we will go out for some fun;' so I went. We went up to a joom, where there were two houses, in which lived a family of two unmarried sisters—a married one with her husband, and the father and mother. When we came there, my companion said to the girls, 'We have come to eat birnee grain;' and they said, 'Come in, and we will cook for you; and I said to him, 'I don't want to eat;' he said, 'You do not understand: when I said we have come to eat birnee, that meant, that we had come to have some fun; if they had been disinclined, they would have said the birnee is not yet ripe; come up, you don't know our customs:' so we went up, and saluted the elders. The house-father had been drinking, and he was merry, and called to me and said, 'How! are you married?' and I said, 'No.' Then he said, laughing, 'If you were married, I should look upon you as good company for me; but as you are a bachelor, you are only good enough for the girls. Quite right: we did the same when we were young.' Presently he and the mother and the married daughter got up and went off to the other house where they slept, and then my companion blew out the light and threw water on the fire. We stayed there all night, to eat 'birnee' grain, that is the polite way of phrasing it; but this is a Kowkdyntsa custom; we have not got it among the Palaingtsa. I stayed some time in the village, and I took a great liking for Pynchainda; so we settled to run away. That night there was to be a feast at her father's house, and she and I were to have a singing match, for she was the best singer in her village, and I also sang well. Many people assembled, and they killed a pig and feasted. Afterwards we two sat in the middle of the room, opposite to each other, with a large tray of fresh flowers between us; and the liquor went round, and we sang. I put much love in my song; so after a time Pynchainda's heart become full, and she stopped singing, and took flowers and put them on my head; and she rose quickly and went away, saying she would fetch water; and I also got up and went after her, at which everybody began to laugh. When we got outside, she left her water-pitcher on the bank of the stream, and we came straight away through the jungle."

At the Mang Rajah's village I was once witness of the proceedings in a divorce case, which are worthy of note. The wife was the complainant. She said she had gone down to the stream about twilight with some other girls and a young man to fetch water; and while they were there, the girls began to laugh and splash water on the young man. Her husband had jealously followed her, and saw the fun from the bank; and he had fallen into a fury and abused the young man, and beaten her before every one. She asked the Chief for a divorce, and would not be pacified, although her husband had now become very humble. It was not the first quarrel of the sort, she said; and a woman could endure anything save a jealous husband: that was not according to their customs. The elders of the village assembled; and after hearing all that was to be said on both sides, they tried to make peace, but in vain; so they decreed that the pair should be shut up alone together in an empty room with no bedding (it was in the cold weather), and they would hear the matter again in the morning. Morning came, and the couple came out still ununited; the woman still begged and prayed for a divorce. On this, the court of elders determined that she had cause, and that a divorce should be granted; but the woman should pay Rs. 30 to her husband as a fine. This sentence was accordingly carried out. Rs. 10 of the fine were spent by the jury in a feast as some recompense for their trouble.

The Khyoungtha speak a provincial dialect of the Arracanese language, which tongue was also the parent stock of the modern Burmese language. The written character is the same as the Burmese. The Arracanese language has strong affinities with the Himalayan and Thibetan dialects. Mr. Brian Hodgson is of opinion (Journal B. Asiatic Society, September 1849) that the Burmese language has sprung from the Thibetan, while he finds that it has much in common with the Singpho and Naga dialects.

The Khyoungtha do not dance together. Their festive gatherings, however, have a most distinctive feature in the "Poie," or travelling theatrical company, which every cold season makes its round to the larger and more wealthy villages. I was present a short time ago at an entertainment of this description, given by one of the Chiefs on the marriage of his son, and to which I was invited. Accordingly, preceded by a lantern, and surrounded by about twenty of the villagers, I took my way about 9 p.m. to the opera-house. The proceedings were carried on under a large awning, which spread over a small grassy plot of land, not far from where I was living. The centre pole was tastefully wreathed with green branches and flowers, amid which, at the foot, were set four large lamps, and a big black earthenware pot holding water for the refreshment of the performers. Round this centre pole was left vacant a circular path—stage, arena—call it what you will; and here the business of the evening was transacted. The whole surrounding space was crammed with men and women, old and young, all sitting in wrapt attention, on mats spread on the ground; every one having in his mouth the inevitable cigar. I saw children four or five years old smoking cheroots nearly as big as themselves. The performers, also, male and female, each had a cigar, which, at emotional passages, was stuck either behind the ear or through the pierced lobe thereof. The orchestra occupied a raised position on my left. Before saying anything of the performance, I must describe this orchestra. The instruments were first and foremost a "shawm,"—I can call it nothing else; not that I know in the least what a shawm is like, but this was the name that at once suggested itself to me on seeing it. It was both in sound and appearance a cross between the clarionet and the trumpet. Its music was anything but disagreeable. Besides, this was a curious clapper of white wood used to emphasize the acrid passages of old age. Lastly, there were the drums, musical drums, positively musical. They were of all sizes, in shape semi-spheres, from the small bell-toned tenor to the deep boomer, dedicated to rage and male choruses. The performer on the drums tuned up his battalion with screws in the most scientific style before commencing: he sat in the middle of a circle of these drums, and was the backbone of the orchestra. I was much struck by the opera itself; there was a style and continuity about it such as I have never before seen in eastern performances.

When I arrived, the circle was occupied by about six male performers, and their acting was ludicrously remindful of the European stage. First, the basso would address himself to the chorus, in "recitativo," accompanied gently by the tuned drums and a small invisible instrument of flute-like sound; then full power would be turned on by the whole company. The story or action of the drama, as it seemed to me, was something after this fashion:—First, the King, with four or five attendant courtiers, is discovered walking in his garden. Bass solo by his Majesty; he bewails the wilfulness of the princess royal, who has set her heart upon the worthless young scamp So-and-so, instead of the admirable match that she might make; grumbling and sympathetic chorus of courtiers follows, all with cheroots in their hands, from which they take furtive puffs at breathing times. The monarch stops for a moment to light his weed at one of the foot-lights, and then commences an aria, expressive of intense vexation of spirit, during which the courtiers wisely retire. Enter then the young scamp of a lover, "Il Primo Tenore," got up in all the height of hill dandyism; the monarch now stalks moodily round the stage, followed by the lover, making gestures of entreaty. This dumb show gives occasion for a wonderful display of musical ability on the part of the shawm, the performer on which surpasses himself, and nearly bursts a blood vessel in his efforts, apparently, to get inside his instrument. A duet follows, in which the infuriated monarch tears from the Tenore's ear the flower which his lady-love had given him; and the first act appropriately closed by the King kicking the lover off the stage. Here, looking about me, I noticed a curious arrangement hanging in front of the orchestra. This consisted of a string attached to two bamboos, set perpendicularly, and held by men on each side. From this string hung pendant about twenty of the most uncouth masks that it ever entered into the mind of man to conceive. Men's faces, devils' heads, with the reverse of a woman's face, horses' heads, human feet and hands, all hanging together in most bizarre confusion. A strange and eerie effect was given to this, by the two bamboos being gently shaken to and fro by the men who held them, thus giving to the line of fantastic images a monotonous and regular swaying motion.

I really did like the music; it had distinct rhythm and tune, while the choruses were sometimes very quaint and jolly. The drums, too, with their different and mellow tones were employed most judiciously, varying in expression and "tempo" to suit the dramatic action of the piece.

The next scene showed the princess and three faithful attendants. She has absconded from her father's house, and they are now wandering in the jungle, waiting for the lover. The female performers were three very pretty girls, and there was besides, one comic male retainer. It was curious to see how closely these girls resembled the pictures of Chinese princesses that one sees on screens and in pictures—dress, figures, and fans, all celestial. The performers, without exception, all played their parts, singing and speaking to each other, and not at the audience. The poor little princess's lament, when she thought herself abandoned by her lover in the jungle, was quite pathetic, and when she sank down on her knees, as though all hope were gone, some of the susceptible female portion of the audience were moved to audible weeping. The comic retainer also was very good; even his walk and attitudes were ludicrous.

The piece, of course, closed in the happy conjunction of the lovers, and the traditional parental blessing.

THE CHUKMA TRIBE.

Although the majority of this tribe do not speak the Arracanese dialect, I have classed them with the Khyoungtha, on account of their similarity of habit in the location of their villages on the banks of the streams, in contradistinction to the other tribes, whom I have called Toungtha, from their living on hills in preference to the low lands.

The name of Chukma is given to this tribe in general by the inhabitants of the Chittagong District, and the largest and dominant section of the tribe recognizes this as its rightful appellation. It is also sometimes spelt Tsakma, or Tsak, or, as it is called in Burmese, Thek. A smaller section of the same tribe is called Doingnak. The names of Chukma, Tsak, Thek, and Doingnak, may all therefore be taken as names representing the tribe of which I now propose to speak. There is a third division, or clan, called Toungjynyas. The origin of the tribe can only be inferred from their traditions and physique, as they possess no written records of ancient times. Intelligent persons among them, however, have informed me that it has been handed down from father to son; that they came originally from a country called Chainpango, or Champanugger. As to where this country is situated accounts vary somewhat. By some it is said to be near Malacca; this would ascribe to them a Malay origin: while, on the other hand, there are many that assert that Champanugger is situated far to the north in the North-Western Provinces of Hindostan[6]. Those who hold to this latter view say that they are descended from a Khettrie family of the name of Chandra. The facial characteristics of the tribe are indicative of Mongolian, and not Aryan extraction; and it is, moreover, only of late years that the use of the Arracanese vernacular has died out among them. The majority of the tribe, however, hold that they are descended from

[6] Champanugger.—Probably the kingdom of Champa, mentioned in the travels of Fa Hian, a Chinese pilgrim, who traversed India in the year 429 of the Christian Era. He speaks of the kingdom of Champa, the capital of which was Campapuri, or Karnopura, situated not far from the site of the present Bhagulpore. (*See* also Bishop Bigandet's *Life of Gaudama*, p. 430, 2nd edition.)

a Hindoo family of good caste. The story they tell is as follows:—The reigning King of Champanugger had two sons; and the elder of these went forth with a picked body of men to attack the King of Mogoda[7]. In the contest he was victorious; but on his turning his face homewards news reached him that his old father had died, and his younger brother had usurped the throne, and was prepared to resist his return. On this the elder brother determined to remain in the country he had newly conquered, and accordingly settled in these hills. His followers took wives from among the country people, who were Buddhists; and to this it is attributable that they forsook the religion of their forefathers, and have altered also somewhat in complexion and appearance. The Khyoungtha, again, have another story of the origin of the Chukma tribes. It is this:—The Chukmas

[7] This, doubtless, refers to Magotha, a country frequently named in Buddhistic writings. It is the country known now as South Behar. Its situation has been well ascertained.

were originally Moguls or Mussulmans. Once the "Wuzeer" of Chittagong collected together an army to attack the King of Arracan; and as the force went travelling over the hills they came to the hut of a Poongyee, a holy man in the wilderness. This Poongyee begged the Wuzeer to halt and partake of some refreshment which he would quickly prepare; and to this the Wuzeer consented. After some time, as the food did not make its appearance, he sent a soldier to the Poongyee's hut to see when it would be ready. The soldier entered the hut and saw that the Poongyee had put rice and flesh in a pot, and had placed the pot over the fire-place; but he noticed with astonishment that there was no wood in the fire-place: instead thereof the Poongyee had put his foot under the pot, and flames were issuing from the tips of his toes. So the soldier returned to the Wuzeer and made his report. On hearing the man's statement the Wuzeer became enraged, and said, "At that rate the rice will never be ready;" and he gave orders for the march to be recommenced. Consequently, when the holy man came out to redeem his pledged hospitality, he found his guest had unceremoniously departed. On this the Poongyee waxed very wroth, and he cursed the Wuzeer and all his army, and sent forth powerful charms after them, so that when they met the King of Arracan's troops their hearts turned to water, and they were all made prisoners. The King of Arracan settled all these Mussulmans as slaves in his territory, and gave them wives of the people of the country; and they increased and multiplied. This was the origin of the Chukma tribe. In corroboration of this story I subjoin a list of the Rajahs who are known to have reigned over the tribe, from which it will be seen that the name of Khan, a purely Pathan patronymic, is commonly in use among them :—

1. Jumaul Khan.	About 1715 A.D. first paid tribute of cotton to Mogul Wuzeer Fumuck Shah.

2. Sheremusta Khan.	
3. Sookdel Roy.	A.D. 1737 made settlement with English Government.
4. Shere Dowlut Khan.	In 1776 he revolted against Government, and two expeditions were sent against him and Ranoo, or Ramoo Khan, his relative, and a chief man of the tribe. (*See* Introduction.)
5. Jaunbux Khan.	A.D. 1782 the cotton tribute reduced to 500 maunds. This chief oppressed the tribe heavily, and many of them fled to Arracan. He also revolted against Government; but in 1787 he made submission. In 1789 the Government determined that the tribute should be paid in money instead of cotton.
6. Tubber Khan.	
7. Jubber Khan.	
8. Dhurmbux Khan.	A.D. 1812, died about 1830.
9. Kalindee Ranee.	The present head of the tribe (a woman).

Mr. Hodgson (Journal Bengal Asiatic

Society, No. I. of 1853) states his opinion that the Thek (Chukma) of Arracan are of aboriginal descent. In this view, however, I cannot concur.

Colonel Phayre treats of the Thek and the Doingnak apparently as if they were two separate tribes. In this idea I venture to think that he is mistaken, as the Doingnaks are known and recognized throughout the tribe as a branch of the Chukmas that abandoned the parent stem during the Chiefship of Jaunbux Khan about 1782. The reason of this split was a disagreement on the subject of marriages. The Chief passed an order that the Doingnak clan should intermarry with the tribe in general. This was contrary to ançient custom, and caused discontent, and eventually a break in the tribe. The Doingnaks, however, are now straggling back, village by village, on their return to the tribe. Several of their villages are found in the Cox Bazar Hills, and they preserve to this day the remembrance of the places inhabited formerly by their ancestors on the Kurnafoolee River, although from long residence in Arracan their vernacular language is the dialect of that country, and they are, comparatively speaking, ignorant of Bengallee, a bastard dialect of which is spoken by the tribe at large. Colonel Phayre (J. A. S., No. 117 of 1841) says of the Doingnaks:—"They call themselves Kheem-ba-nago. Of their descent I could learn nothing; probably they may be the offspring of Bengallees carried into the hills as slaves, where their physical appearance has been modified by change of climate. In religion they are Buddhists." Whatever opinion may be formed of the primal origin of the Thek, or Chukma tribe, no doubt can exist as to their having been at one time inhabitants of the province of Arracan, from whence they have migrated to these hills. The Radza-wong, or History of the Arracan Kings, gives the following account of them. It is there written that King Kaumysing, the son of the King of Baranathi, having been assigned by his father, as heritage, all the country inhabited by the Burman, Shan, and

Malay races, came to Ramawati, the ancient capital of Arracan, near the modern town of Sandoway. He there collected men from the different countries of Western Hindoostan, having a variety of languages. They then asking for subsistence; to the first who so applied he gave the name of Thek, and their language being different from the rest, they lived separate. The Thek tribe appears afterwards to have played a part of some importance in the annals of the kingdom. King Nya-ming-nya-tain, with the help of the Tsaks, is said to have gained the throne in the year 356 of the Arracan Era. Again, in 656, King Mengdi is said to have undertaken an expedition against the Shans and Tsaks, who had become very troublesome (Phayre's History of Arracan, J. A. S., No. 145 of 1844). The tribe is also mentioned by Buchanan in his paper on the religion and literature of the Burmese (Asiatic Researches, Vol. VI., p. 229). The Toungjynya section of the tribe, to the number of 4000 souls, is said to have come into the Chittagong Hills, as late as 1819, in the time of the Chief Dhurmbux Khan. They acknowledge as their head one Phahproo, but Dhurmbux Khan would not recognize him as head of the Toungjynya clan, and consequently the major part of them returned to Arracan. At the present time the Toungjynyas in this district are said to number 2500 souls. The elders among them are still acquainted with the Arracanese vernacular, but the present generation are fast amalgamating with the rest of the tribe, and use with them a corrupt species of Bengallee. Some few words are in general use among the Chukmas, which are apparently derived neither from Arracanese nor Bengallee roots, and from which possibly some clue may be gained as to their origin. My collection, however, is very scanty; and a closer acquaintance with their dialect would perhaps give more ample and satisfactory results.

Lyngia,	a lover.
Langonee,	a mistress.
Sowalta,	best man at wedding.
Sowullee,	bridesmaid.

Ojha,	an exorcist,	
Tagul,	a dâo, or hill knife.	
Mooi,	I.	
Bey,	sister.	
Siggun Bey,	little sister.	
Boojee,	elder brother's wife.	
Moozee,	mother's younger sister.	
Jeydee,	mother's elder sister.	
Sillum,	a jacket.	
Khadee,	woman's breast-cloth.	
Rain-ya,	an abandoned joom.	Arracanese ya, a joom, or field of hill cultivation.
Moyn	a hill.	
Masmoola,	about a month.	Mas (Bengallee), a month.
Goza,	clan or family.	

They have a written character peculiar to the tribe, but the form of the letters show that they are merely a rude adaptation of the Arracanese alphabet.

The tribe is said to contain about 25,000 souls exclusive of the Arracan offshoots. The Chukmas Proper, as distinguished from the Toungjynya and Doingnaks, whom they largely outnumber, are divided into 21 Gozas, or clans. In calling to a Chukma, one does not ask him his caste, that is shown by his face and dress; but it is usual to demand, "Of what Goza are you?"

Over each Goza there is a Dewan, who represents the head of the family, from which his clan originally sprung. Among the Toung-jynyas this hereditary head is called the Ahoon. He collects the poll-tax (the sole hill revenue), and, retaining a certain fixed proportion thereof, pays the remainder to the Chief of the tribe, together with a yearly offering of first-fruits. He has the privilege of deciding cases, and for so doing receives certain fees, the amount of which is prescribed by custom (of these more hereafter). The Dewan also receives as a right a portion of any wild animal, fit for food, that may be killed by any of his people. When the Goza is a large one, the Dewan appoints several subordinates under him to assist in the administration; these officers are called "Khejas." They are exempt from the payment of revenue, and from the "corvée," or unpaid labour, to which the rest of the tribe are liable; but every year they are bound to present to their Dewan an offering of one measure of rice, one bamboo tube of spirits, and one fowl. Their office does not appear to be hereditary.

The religion professed by the Chukma tribe is Buddhism; but their propinquity to, and constant contact with, the Bengallees, has caused them to mingle with their pure and æsthetic rites much that appertains to Hindoo superstition. They have not as yet imbibed, I am thankful to say, any prejudices as to caste, but many signs and tokens manifest their gravitation towards Hindooism. They have for the most part abandoned the Arracanese vernacular; they observe the Luckhee and Doorga Poojahs, both purely Hindoo festivals. They consult Hindoo astrologers, and have begun to find out that they are descended from the caste of Khettries in Hindoostan.

They observe eight festivals of their own during the year.

These holy times are common to, and observed alike by, both the Khyoungtha and the Chukmas; and it may be that they are followed by Buddhists generally: but on this point I am not able, neither is it necessary, for me to speak. The Bishoo is the chief festival in the year. At that time, as I have previously described, all classes, men and women alike, resort to the Mahamuni temple to make offerings at the shrine of Gaudama, to give gifts to each other, and rejoice. This festival occurs in the month of April. In the month of July the Sadhang begins. This is a time of fasting, when persons who wish to do meritorious actions give alms, and bind themselves by a vow to abstain from some particular pleasure, such as good eating, fine clothes, their wife's society, or the like. The fast continues for three months; and for that period the priests are bound to remain stationary at whatever place they may be, and continuously to recite the law and chant the praises of Gaudama. The Tummungtong is a feast at the close of this fast. Magiri is a time of festival when the rice begins to ripen, and when prayers are offered up that no harm may befall the crop. The Hoia and Nowarno occur in October. This is a season of much feasting, corresponding to our harvest home. The Chukmas at this season have a curious custom of suspending seven breast-cloths (worn by their women) from a lofty pole erected in the village, at the foot of which sacrifice is offered. This is the time of eating the new rice. The Kheyrey and Tsoomoolang are festivals of minor importance, and of no fixed date. The Shongbasa is the worship of the "nats," or deities of wood and stream. The priests have nothing to do with this, and it has been condemned as an unorthodox practice. The sacrifice is either offered by the votary himself in person, or an "ojha," or exorcist, is called in to perform the necessary ceremonies.

At a Chukma village I was once present when sacrifice was thus offered up by the head man. The occasion was a thank-offering for the recovery of his wife from childbirth. The offering consisted of a sucking pig and a fowl. The altar was of bamboo decorated with young plantain shoots and leaves. On this raised platform were placed small cups containing rice, vegetables, and a spirit distilled from rice. Round the whole from the house-mother's distaff had been spun a long white thread, which encircled the altar, and then, carried into the house, was held at its two ends by the good man's wife. The sacrifice commenced by a long invocation uttered by the husband, who stood opposite to his altar, and between each snatch of his charm he tapped the small platform with his hill knife, and uttered a long wailing cry; this was for the purpose of attracting the numerous wandering spirits who go up and down upon the earth, and calling them to the feast. When a sufficient number of these invisible guests were believed to be assembled, he cut the throats of the victims with his "dâo," and poured a libation of blood upon the altar and over the thread. The flesh of the things sacrificed was afterwards cooked and eaten at the household meal, of which I was invited to partake.

The social customs of the Chukmas are on the whole very similar to those of the Khyoungtha.

When a child is born the mother is looked upon as impure for one month afterwards. A male child is preferred to a female. On the birth of a son guns are fired, and a feast is given; not so when a daughter is brought into the world. There seem to be no particular ceremonies in the naming of a child; a name is usually given that has been borne by some ancestor. Children are generally suckled by their mothers for a long time; it is not uncommon to see a boy of three years old sharing his mother's milk with a young infant. Girls reach puberty at the age of thirteen, and boys at fourteen to fifteen years. When a lad becomes fit, he goes out to cut his first joom; this is a sign of manhood among them, and the parents are bound in honour to give a feast to all their relatives on this occasion. Child marriages among the

Chukmas, or indeed among the hill people in general, are unknown; there is no fixed time for getting married. Some of the young men indeed do not marry until they reach the age of twenty-four or twenty-five; after that age, however, it is rare to see a man unmarried. Marriage is after this fashion. Father, mother, and son, first look about them and fix upon a bride; this indispensable preliminary accomplished, the parents go to the house where their intended daughter-in-law resides. They take with them a bottle of spirits (this is an absolute necessary in every hill palaver). The matter will at first be opened cautiously; the lad's father will say, "That is a fine tree growing near your house, I would fain plant in its shadow." Should all go well, they retire after mutual civilities. Both in going and coming, omens are carefully observed; and many a promising match has been put a stop to by unfavourable auguries. A man or woman carrying fowls, water, fruit, or milk, if passed on the right hand, is a good omen, and pleasant to meet with;

but it is unfavourable to see a kite or a vulture, or to see one crow all by himself, croaking on the left hand. If they are unfortunate enough to come upon the dead body of any animal on their road, they will go no further, but at once return home and stop all proceedings. Old people quote numerous stories to show that the disregard of unfavourable omens has in former times been productive of the most ruinous consequences.

By the time a second visit is due, the relatives on both sides have been consulted; and if all has progressed satisfactorily, and there are no dissentient voices, they go accompanied by some of the girls of the village, taking with them presents of curds and "birnee" grain, and "jogra," a sweet fermented liquor made from rice. Then a day is settled (after the harvest is a favourite time), and a ring of betrothal is given to the bride. Now also is arranged what price the young man is to pay for his wife, for the Chukmas, in contradistinction to all our other tribes, buy their wives. The ordinary price is 100 to 150 rupees. On the marriage day a large stock of provisions is laid in by both houses. A procession of men and women starts from the bridegroom's village with drums and music to fetch home the bride. The parents of the bridegroom present their intended daughter with her marriage dress. No ceremony, however, is performed; and the bride, after a short interval, is taken away, accompanied by all her relatives to her new home.

On arriving all enter the house, and the bride and bridegroom sit down together at a small table—the bride on the left hand of her husband. On the table are eggs, sweetmeats, rice, and plantains, all laid out on leaf platters. The best man (sowalla) sits behind the bridegroom, and the bride has a representative bridesmaid (sowallee) behind her. These two then bind around the couple a muslin scarf, asking, "Are all willing, and shall this thing be accomplished?" Then all cry out, "Bind them, bind them:" so they are bound. The married pair have now to eat together, the wife feeding the husband

and the husband the wife; and as at this stage of the ceremony a great deal of bashfulness is evinced, the bridesmaid and best man raise the hands of their respective charges to and from each other's mouths, to the intense enjoyment and hilarity of every one present. After they have thus eaten and drunken, an elder of the village sprinkles them with river water, pronounces them man and wife, and says a charm used for fruitfulness. The couple then retire, and the guests keep it up until an early hour on the following morning. The next day, at the morning meal, the newly married come hand-in-hand and salute the elders of their families. The father of the bride generally improves this occasion by addressing a short lecture to his son-in-law on the subject of marital duties. "Take her," he says, "I have given her to you; but she is young and not acquainted with her household duties. If therefore at any time you come back from the joom and find the rice burnt, or any thing else wrong, teach her, do not beat her; but at the end of three years, if she still continues ignorant, then beat her, but do not take her life, for if you do I shall demand the price of blood at your hands; but for beating her I shall not hold you responsible, or interfere."

All marriages, however, do not go on in this happy fashion; it often happens that the lad and the lass have made up their minds to couple, but the parents will not hear of the match. In such a case the lovers generally elope together; but should the girl's parents be very much set against the match, they have the right to demand back and take their daughter from the hands of her lover. If, notwithstanding this opposition, the lovers' intentions still remain unaltered, and they elope a second time, no one has then the right to interfere with them. The young husband makes a present to his father-in-law according to his means, gives a feast to his new relatives, and is formally admitted into kinship.

These elopements in the hills are sometimes the occasion of tragical consequences.

A case in point happened in the district the other day among the Chukmas.

A young man, named Boopeea, was in love with a girl called Shonia-mullah. The girl lived with her old father (her mother was dead) and one brother named Heeradhun. It was joom time, and they all lived together, away from the village, in the lonely little house which it is the custom for each family to build in their own joom (this reminds one of Isaiah's solitary "lodge in a garden of cucumbers"). An elder brother, named Jooradhun, lived separately down in the village. He was married. Boopeea loved the girl, and could not keep away from her. He was constantly hanging about the house, helping in the joom, and eating and sleeping in the common room of the house. He was too poor to make the legitimate proposals to the girl's relatives, for this course would entail numerous heavy expenses, besides a cash payment of at least 40 rupees. For two years he hung about her, and she loved him. At last they agreed to elope. The rest of the story is best told in the words of Heeradhun, the girl's brother:—

"Last Friday, when I came home from work, my father said to me, 'Where is your sister? She went out some time ago to fetch water and has not returned. I suspect she has run off at last with that worthless fellow Boopeea, who is always hanging about the house.' On this I went and called two or three other young men who lived close by, and we went off after my sister. We met her and Boopeea in the valley by the stream. Boopeea was first in the path; my sister followed after him holding his hand. Then I was enraged, and I ran at Boopeea and cut at him with my dâo: he leapt on one side, and the blow fell on my sister. She said once, 'Oh brother!' and then fell dead. The dâo cut her side open. Then I was frightened and ran away. I knew nothing positive of Shonia and Boopeea being in love, although I suspected it: it is not our custom to make public our love affairs. If Boopeea had applied to the family, and been able to pay the usual sums of money, we would have consulted together, and given him our sister in marriage. He would not have spoken himself; he would have employed a third party: but as he was unable to pay the necessary expenses, he ran away with her. It is our custom, in elopements, for the young men of the village to go in search of the runaway couple. If they catch them, they ask the girl whether she leaves her home voluntarily, or whether force has been used. In the former case she is let go, but her husband has afterwards to pay a fine. If they are not caught, they get off free, and the elders settle it according to custom."

Among the Toungjynya and Doingnak sections of the tribe, the unmarried lads are all assembled at night in one house under the charge of an elder lad, in the same way as in the Khyoungtha villages. This, however, is not the custom with the Chukmas Proper. The lads play at "konyon," as described among the Khyoungtha; the game is known to them as "geela kara." They also play a game resembling our English "touch." Peg-top is a common amusement among them. Cards, dice, or gambling for money, are unknown. The Jew's-harp has, on its late introduction, gained a high place in the estimation of the junior portion of the community.

In one point in particular the Chukmas differ from the whole of the other hill tribes, viz., that they are averse from changing the sites of their villages. From generation to generation the village is kept at one place; but yet they do not aim at any permanency of structure, the houses being built in hill fashion, of bamboo only, thatched with leaves.

The custom of putting a village in quarantine in case of sickness is universal amongst them. The average duration of life, they say, does not run beyond sixty years, but that formerly disease was much less common among them, and it was not unusual to find men and women attain the age of 90 or even 100 years. They instance, in proof of this, three diseases which have appeared among them within the last two generations:—First, a sickness called "tsana peera." This disease appears first in the form of a low intermittent fever; but the attacks increase in frequency until the type changes to remittent, the tongue and throat become ulcerated, delirium sets in, and is followed by death. Second, "noa-bees," or the new poison; this is simply a strong remittent fever. Both these diseases are said to have been unknown until within the last sixty years, and I can quite believe this to be true, as the wilder hill tribes, further east, still enjoy immunity from these attacks. The third disease, which has only lately made its appearance among them, is syphilis. They are well acquainted with herbs and simples, and possess a rough pharmacy of their own; but they have no medicine-men, professionally speaking. The dress of the Chukmas is similar to that of the Khyoungtha, save that the petticoat of the women is of coarse blue and red home-spun, and is worn rather shorter. Their jewellery also is somewhat different in shape.

They burn their dead. In the case of a

man, the body is burnt with its face to the east, and five layers of wood are used; while a woman is burnt face westward, and seven layers of wood are consumed in the funeral pile. Both the Chukmas and Khyoungtha use more wood to burn the dead body of a woman than of a man, and this is curious, as one would imagine that from the greater development of fatty and cellular tissue in women, less combustibles would be required.

On the death of a Dewan or of a priest a curious sport is customary at the funeral. The corpse is conveyed to the place of cremation on a car; to this car ropes are attached, and the persons attending the ceremony are divided into two equal bodies and set to work to pull in opposite directions. One side represents the good spirits; the other, the powers of evil. The contest is so arranged that the former are victorious. Sometimes, however, the young men representing the demons are inclined to pull too vigorously, but a stick generally quells this unseemly ardour in the cause of evil. If possible, at the close of a funeral, there is a display of fireworks, and guns are discharged. If a man is believed to have died from witchcraft, the body, when half burned, is divided down the chest. A post, pole, or some other portion of the dead man's house is usually burned with him. The ashes of the pile are thrown into the river, by the side of which cremation invariably takes place. At the burning place the relatives erect a lofty pole with a long streamer of coarse cloth pendent therefrom. Seven days after death, as among the Khyoungtha, the priests assemble to read prayers for the dead, and the relatives give alms.

Crime of any sort is rare amongst the Chukmas; the most frequent misdemeanours are those connected with women, and for these a certain scale of fines is allotted. The said fines are divided between the Chief of the tribe and the head man or Dewan.

If a man runs away with another man's wife, he has to repay to the injured husband all the former expenses of marriage, and is fined 40 to 60 rupees. Should near relatives (within certain prohibited degrees) fall in love with each other, it is usual for both of them to pay a fine of 50 rupees, and corporal punishment is also administered.

Divorce is not difficult of attainment amongst them, and can be awarded by a jury of village elders. The party who is judged to be in fault is fined heavily. As a rule, however, divorce is uncommon, and the women make good and faithful wives.

In serious cases, where the guilt or innocence of any person is to be tested, they use the ordeal by rice. A seer of rice is put into a pot and left all night before the shrine of Gaudama at one of the temples; in the morning the elders assemble, and the supposed culprit is called upon to chew some of this rice. If he is innocent, he finds no difficulty in doing so; but if justly accused, he is not only unable to masticate the rice, but blood is believed to issue from his mouth. In a case like this a very heavy fine is exacted. In default of payment of fine, the culprit ought, according to old custom, to become a slave for such time as will enable him to work off the penalty.

The abduction of a young girl against her will is punished by a fine of 60 rupees, and the offender also receives a good beating from the lads of the village to which the girl belongs. Theft is unknown among the Chukmas, and formerly they settled all their disputes among themselves. Of late years, however, a spirit of litigation has grown up among them, and they now resort to our courts more than any other tribe. The Chukmas allow no songs to be sung in or near their villages save those of a religious character; love songs, they say, demoralize the young girls. In the joom, or jungle, however, the tongue is free. They are famous for their flute-playing. Their instrument is simple enough, being merely a joint of bamboo pierced with holes; but from this rough medium they evoke wondrously soft music. I have often, by the river side, listened to the wild, melancholy notes of some unseen player.

"Sweet, sweet, sweet, O Pan!
Piercing sweet by the river!
Blinding sweet, O great god Pan!
The sun on the hill forgot to die,
And the lilies revived, and the dragon-fly
Came back to dream on the river."

PART III.

THE HILL TRIBES (SONS OF THE RIVER).

Continued.

THE tribes to be noticed under this head are—

A.	1. The Tipperahs, or Mroongs. 2. The Kumi, or Kweymee. 3. Mroos. 4. Khyengs.	B.	1. The Bungees. 2. Pankhos.
		C.	1. The Lhoosai, or Kookies. 2. The Shendoos, or Lakheyr.

Of the three subdivisions, A, B, and C, the tribes mentioned under A are tributary to us and entirely subject to our control. Those included in B, although paying no revenue, are subject to our influence; while the tribes mentioned under C are entirely independent.

These tribes are in every respect wilder than the Khyoungtha; they are more purely savages, and unamenable to the lures of civilization. Alcohol and tobacco, the two great speech solvents, they have among them already, and indeed they are independent of all external assistance, the earth supplying them with every necessary of their simpler life. As civilization advances, they will retire, and it will be found, I think, difficult, if not impossible, to wean them from their savage life. The above remarks do not apply to the first-mentioned tribe; for the Tipperahs, although assimilating in manners and customs with the remainder of the Toungtha, are entirely different in character, and are the only hill people, in truth, among whom I have met with meanness and lying, the only people whose savagery is unredeemed by simplicity and manly independence.

The Toungtha are distinguished from the Khyoungtha in many ways. Their villages are, generally speaking, situated on lofty hills and in places difficult of access. The men wear hardly any clothes at all, and the petticoat of the women is scanty, reaching barely below the knee, while their bosoms are left uncovered after the birth of the first child; previous to that the unmarried girls wear a narrow breast-cloth. Both men and women are much given to dancing together. The women do not hold so high a position among them as among the Khyoungtha, and upon them falls the greater part of the labour of life.

Their religion is simple: it is the religion of nature. They worship the terrene elements, and have vague and undefined ideas of some divine power which overshadows all. They were born and they die, for ends to them as incomputable as the path of a cannon-shot fired into the darkness. They are cruel, and attach but little value to life. Reverence or respect are emotions unknown to them; they salute neither their chiefs nor their elders; no form of greeting exists in their many tongues; neither have they any expression conveying thanks. The mainsprings of their existence are hunger, fear, and that sexual impulse which is common to every mere proletarian animal.

They attach importance to an oath; it is with them a rude test or touchstone in matters pertaining to crime, and by which they ratify engagements. The oath is made upon the things upon which their very existence may be said to depend, viz., water, cotton, rice, and the "dâo," or hill knife. They are monogamists, and, as a rule, are faithful husbands and good fathers after marriage. Great license is allowed before marriage to the youth of both sexes, between whom intercourse is entirely unchecked. This practice, however immoral as we should consider it, produces no evil effects among them, but, on the contrary, acts rather beneficially than otherwise. For a man or woman to be unmarried after the age of thirty is unheard of; prostitution is a thing not understood, or, if explained, regarded by them with abhorrence. They draw rightly a strong distinction between a woman prostituting herself habitually as a means of livelihood, and the intercourse by mutual consent of two members of opposite sexes leading, as it generally does, to marriage. Venereal diseases are unknown among them. Marriage with them is more a civil contract than a religious ceremony or sacrament. It is entered into by the mutual agreement of the contracting parties, and can be dissolved at their joint request. Divorce, however, if applied for by one of the parties only, cannot be obtained save by payment of an almost prohibitive fine. Adultery among the wilder tribes is punished by death. Concubinage among them is regarded as disgraceful; and although slavery is a recognized institution among them, yet it is not considered right for a master to take advantage of his position with regard to the female slaves in his house. A master's slaves are his children, and are universally treated well. Should a man's wife die, he may marry one of his slaves; his so doing at once raises her to the position and privileges of a free woman. Slaves are in all cases captives taken in war; the system of debtor slavery, prevailing among the Khyoungtha, is unknown among the wilder tribes.

The position of Chief among them carries with it no great power or privileges. They pay no revenue to their Chief, but he is entitled to receive from each house yearly one basket of rice and one jar of seepah (fermented drink); his share also of the spoils of war is the largest. Each village is a small state, owing fealty and allegiance to no one save their own special leader. A man may leave one Chief, and transfer himself and his family to the village of another; hence it happens that the power of different Chiefs, which depends upon the size of their respective villages, varies considerably from time to time, according to their success or popularity.

They enjoy, as a rule, comparative immunity from the diseases which afflict the people of the plains; and on the only occasions when they have suffered from the scourges of small-pox and cholera, the diseases have been conveyed to them by Bengallees from the plains. The average duration of age is from seventy to eighty years; but it is by no means uncommon to see among them white-haired and bowed old men, of whose age all count has been lost. Women die at a comparatively early age, owing to the constant labour which their sex entails upon them. There is but one medicine current among all the Toungtha; this is the dried gall bladder and the dung of the boa-constrictor, which is supposed to be, and is used as, a remedy for everything. Amber, however, is greatly prized among them, and is worn as a necklace; but I cannot say whether it is believed to possess any curative powers. Sacrifices are also offered by them in cases of sickness, to avert the anger of some special deity of wood or vale, who is supposed to have sent the disease. If their offerings prove unavailing, they conclude either that they have not hit upon the right deity, or that he is implacable and refuses to be appeased.

In cases of epidemics, the custom of quarantine, or, as it is called, "khang," is universal among them. The quarantine is inaugurated and declared with a certain degree of ceremony. A sacrifice is offered, and the village is encircled with a fresh-spun white thread. The blood of the animal sacrificed is then sprinkled about the village, and a general sweeping and cleansing takes place, the houses and gates being decorated with green boughs. They attach great importance to the quarantine being kept unbroken. It generally lasts three days, and during that time no one is allowed to enter or leave the village. I have known several murders committed, owing to persons persisting in breaking the "khang." The intoxicating liquors used by them are of three kinds, viz., khoung, a sweet fermented liquor made from rice; seepah, a fermented liquor made from "birnee" grain; and arrack, that is alcohol, distilled from rice. Opium, ganja, bhang, and other stimulants, are as yet unknown to them.

There are four clans of the Tipperah tribe resident in the Chittagong Hill Tracts, as follow:—The Pooran, the Nowuttea, the

Osuie, and the Reeang. All came originally from Hill Tipperah.

According to the report of the Trigonometrical Survey, Hill Tipperah is situated between the plains of the British District of Tipperah and the Chatterchoora Range south of Cachar, and consists of five ranges of hills, which run almost parallel with each other from north to south. Below Lat. 23° 48′, these ranges are connected by transverse branches, which separate the head waters of the streams flowing north into the Barak River, from those of the Goomtee flowing west into British Tipperah, and the Fenny and Kurnafoolee flowing into the Chittagong District.

The origin of the name of Tipperah is doubtful. It is pronounced and spelt in Bengallee, "Tripoora." The Sanscrit term "Tripoorardana" is used to indicate the sun; and as judging by the remains of a temple dedicated to the sun, which exist at Odeypara, the ancient capital of Tipperah, the worship of the sun seems to have formed part of the *cultus* of Hill Tipperah; it is not an improbable hypothesis to suppose that the name Tipperah is derived from "Tripoorardana," the sun god. The name of Tipperah, however, is, I believe, an appellation of purely Bengallee derivation. The people themselves, in their own tongue, recognize no generic term by which their race may be designated. If you ask a man of what race he is, he will tell you the name of his clan, Pooran, Osuie, or whatever it may be; but if he is speaking Bengallee, he will use the generic term Tipperah.

The country of Hill Tipperah is governed by a Rajah. He calls himself a Hindoo of the Khettrie caste; but the people themselves say that he is descended from their blood and bone, "otherwise how should we pay him tribute." The Rajah, however, has become, to all intents and purposes, a Hindoo; and a crowd of needy parasites of that religion surround him, and are the agents by which his country is administered. These proceedings are naturally not approved by the bulk of his people, and consequently a yearly emigration takes place from Hill Tipperah into the Chittagong Hills; and we now possess a large population of Tipperahs, numbering some 15,000 souls.

The Tipperahs for the most part live in the country to the north of the River Kurnafoolee. The hills bordering on Hill Tipperah are principally inhabited by the Pooran and Nowuttea clans. Reeangs are the wildest of all, and live in close juxtaposition with the independent tribes of Lhoosai (or Kookies) on our eastern frontier. The Osuie are a comparatively small and scattered clan; some of their villages are found near the Fenny River; some on the hills near the Kurnafoolee; while two of their villages have gone southward into the Bohmong's country, and have cultivated on the Dollookhyoung, a tributary of the River Sungoo. Like all the hill tribes the village community, governed by the head man, or Roaja, is the leading characteristic of their social polity. They cultivate in the usual manner by jooming.

Their villages, however, do not stay long in one place: they are a restless people. The Tipperahs are passionately fond of dancing, and at the time of their great harvest festival, which takes place generally in November, the dances are kept up sometimes for two days and two nights without intermission. The dances are in every way seemly, although the drinking of seepah and "khoung" (sweet fermented liquor made from rice) is enormous. Drunkenness among them, however, does not take an amorous or a pugnacious direction; it generally expends itself in vehement dancing, until such time as the head becomes giddy, and the dancer lies down to sleep off what he has drunk. When the dance begins it is the custom for the old men and women of the village to lead off, and after they have retired the young people have their fling.

Great freedom of intercourse is allowed between the sexes; but a Tipperah girl is never known to go astray out of her own clan. An illegitimate birth, also, is hardly known among them, for the simple reason that, should a girl become *enceinte*, her lover has to marry her. The girls are totally free from the prudery that distinguishes Mahommedan and Hindoo women, and they have an open, frank manner, combined with a womanly modesty that is attractive. At a marriage there is no particular ceremony, but a great deal of drinking and dancing. A pig is killed as a sacrifice to the deities of the wood and stream, the crowning point of the affair being this:—the girl's mother pours out a glass of liquor and gives it to her daughter, who goes and sits on her lover's knee, drinks half, and gives him the other half; they afterwards crook together their little fingers. If a match be made with the consent of the parents, the young man has to serve three years in his father-in-law's house before he obtains his wife or is formally married. During the period of probation his sweetheart is, to all intents and purposes, a wife to him. On the wedding night, however, the bridegroom has to sleep with his wife surreptitiously, entering the house by stealth, and leaving it before dawn. He then absents himself for four days, during which time he makes a round of visits among all his friends. On the fourth day he is escorted back with great ceremony, and has to give another feast to his *cortége*. A Tipperah widow may re-marry if it so seems good to her. Every lad before marriage has his sweetheart, and he cohabits with her whenever opportunity serves; this, however, is without the knowledge of the elders. I once asked a young man whether he was not afraid of his *liaison* coming to the knowledge of the girl's relatives. He replied, "No, it is the custom; what can they say? they did the same when they were young, and their daughter is responsible for her own actions. She likes me and I like her."

The following story is illustrative of their customs and feelings in this respect. I took it down from the lips of a handsome young Tipperah of the Reeang clan:—

"Once in our village it was harvest time, and we were all to go to Chomteyah's joom to gather in the grain. At early morning we all started—all the lads and lasse of the village. Among the girls was one pretty young creature, about fourteen years old; her name was Bamoyntee. I had never seen her before; her father and mother had just come from another village, and settled in ours, where they had relatives. On the road I could not take my eyes from off her—she was so pretty. I spoke to her, but she would answer nothing save yes or no. Some of the other girls noticed us, and they began teasing me and laughing. When we got to the joom, before setting to work, some one had to be chosen to cook the midday meal, which is eaten on the spot; so they all laughed at us a great deal, and chose Bamoyntee and me, and said to us, 'Go you two, and gather vegetables, and come back quickly to cook.' Then I was glad, and said to her, 'Come,' but she would not walk with me; she walked at some distance away. I had my dâo, and she carried a small basket slung at her back; so we went down the hill into the bed of a small stream, but I never thought about vegetables; I thought about her only. She began looking for young vegetables, the tender shoots of the fern, the sprouts of young canes, and other things that grow wild. I was ashamed; I did not know what to say. Presently, as we were going along in the cool bed of the stream, with the trees meeting over our heads, she saw a beautiful pink orchid growing high up on the branch of a forest tree, and she said, 'Oh, I wish I had that!' So I threw down my dâo, and climbed to get the flower. Our Reeang girls prize this sort of flower much, and wear it in their hair. I soon got up the tree; but the branch on which the flower grew was rotten, and broke with me, and I fell down from a great height, and lost my senses. When I woke I found her crying, and bathing my face with water from the stream; and I said to her, 'O Bamoyntee, do not be angry, and I will say something!' She answered, 'Speak.' I said, 'You won't be angry?' And she answered, 'No;' and she took the flower that was in my hand. So I said, 'I love you;' and she hid her face, and I took her in my arms and said, 'Answer me—you are not angry?' She said, 'No.' So I asked her, 'Do you love me?' And she whispered, 'Yes;' and I said, 'Then why did you not tell me so?' She replied, 'It is not the custom for women to speak first; I was ashamed.' Then I said, 'May I come to your father's house to-night?' And she answered, 'Come; but now we must be quick and gather vegetables, or they will laugh at us when we get back.' So we made haste and got vegetables, and went back to the joom. When we got there, the young men and maidens began laughing, and said, 'Well, have you come to an understanding, you two?—is it all settled?' But we said nothing in reply. When the sun was sinking, and the baskets filled with corn-ears, we all set off homewards. I delayed, on one pretence and another, until I was left behind, and she saw this; but at last they all went off singing. She loitered and fell back on the way, so we two went home together. She said to me, 'Come to-night to my father's house before we sleep, so that you may see where I spread my mat.' When we got near the village she went on alone, and I made a circuit through the jungle, and came in at the other side of the village where our house was. At nightfall I went to her house, and her parents received me kindly, and brought out the arrack, and I ate with them, but I said nothing. Afterwards we sat and smoked our pipes. I was determined that I would not go away until I had seen where Bamoyntee spread her mat; and at the last she was ashamed, and would not spread it till her mother got angry and rated her, saying, 'Come, my daughter, you are lazy to-night; spread the mats, for it is time to sleep.' Then I saw the place where she slept, and I went away. At midnight I got up, and came softly back to the house. I went up the ladder to the door, and was just going in, when their great dog came at me, barking; but Bamoyntee came to the door and quieted him. Then I took her hand, and we went in together, keeping step as we walked, like one person. I slept there that night and many nights afterwards, till at last the old people called me son; and I left my father's house, and lived there for good. She is my wife now."

The dress of the Tipperahs is of the simplest description. Among the men a thick turban is worn, and a narrow piece of homespun cloth, with a fringed end hanging down in front and rear, passes once round the waist and between the legs. In the cold season they wear a rudely-sewn jacket. The males wear silver earrings, crescent-shaped, with little silver pendants on the outer edge. The dress of the women is equally unornate. The petticoat is short, reaching a little below the knee, and made of very coarse cotton stuff of their own manufacture. It is striped in colours of red and blue. If the woman be married, this petticoat will form her whole costume; but the unmarried girls cover the breast with a gaily-dyed cloth with fringed ends. The women never cover their heads; they wear earrings like the men; but in addition to this ornament they distend the lobe of the ear to the size of half a crown by the insertion of a concave-edged ring of silver, placed, not through, but in the lobe. Both sexes have long, black, abundant hair, which is worn in a knot at the back of the head. The use of false hair is common among them, especially the women. The meshes of false hair are woven in among the back hair to make the knot look larger.

The Tipperahs make use of an ingenious device to obtain fire; they take a piece of dry bamboo about a foot long, split it in half, and on its outer round surface cut a nick or notch, about an eighth of an inch broad, circling round the semi-circumference of the bamboo, shallow towards the edges, but deepening in the centre, until a minute slit of about a line in breadth pierces the inner surface of the bamboo fire-stick. Then a flexible slip of bamboo is taken, about 1½ feet long and an eighth of an inch in breadth, to fit the circling notch or groove in the fire-stick. This slip or band is rubbed with fine dry sand, and then passed round the fire-stick, on which the operator stands, a foot on either end. Then the slip, grasped firmly, an end in each hand, is pulled steadily back and forth, increasing gradually in pressure and velocity as the smoke comes. By the time the fire-band snaps with the friction, there ought to appear through the slit in the fire-stick some incandescent dust, and this, placed smouldering as it is, in a nest of dry bamboo shavings, can be gently blown into a flame. At night, in camping out in the jungle, they adopt a novel precaution to prevent the dew from the trees dripping on them.

The trunk of the tree under which they intend to rest is notched upwards with a dâo. This, they say, causes the tree to absorb all the dew that falls on it, and the leaves will not drip. On rising in the morning, the operation must be reversed, and the tree knotched seven times with the dâo, edge earthwards, otherwise they say that the spirits of the wood would be offended, and both the tree and those who slept beneath it would die. Another characteristic trait of theirs I remember. We were travelling once through the jungles, and the path led across a small streamlet. Here I observed a white thread stretched from one side to the other, bridging the stream. On inquiring the reason of this, it appeared that a man had died away from his home in a distant village; his friends had gone thither and performed his obsequies, after which it was supposed that the dead man's spirit would accompany them back to his former abode. Without assistance, however, spirits are unable to cross running water; therefore the stream here had been bridged in the manner aforesaid.

Divorce can be obtained among the Tipperahs as among all the hill tribes, on the adjudication of a jury of village elders. One such case I remember to have seen. The divorce was sued for by the wife, on the ground of habitual cruelty. The jury deliberated and found that the cruelty was proved, and that the divorce should be granted. Some check, however, they determined must be put upon the women, or otherwise every wife would complain if her husband raised his little finger at her. Accordingly they gave sentence that the divorce was granted; but that as the woman was wrong to insist upon abandoning her lawful husband, she should give up all her silver ornaments to him, pay a fine of 30 rupees, and provide a pig with trimmings, in the shape of ardent spirits, to be discussed by the jury.

In disputes among the Tipperahs, where one man asserts a thing and the other denies it, I have frequently seen the matter decided at the request of both parties by the hill oath on the dâo, rice, cotton, and river water. I remember one case in which two men disputed as to the ownership of a cow; both parties claiming the animal: at last the man who wished to get possession of the beast said, "Well, if he will swear by the dâo that the cow has always been in his possession and is his property, I will abandon all claim." The other man agreed to this, and took the required oath; after which both parties retired quite satisfied, the man at whose instance the oath was taken, remarking that the result now was in the hands of the deities.

The Tipperah village system is the same as that of the Khyoungthas; there is a village head man chosen by the residents, through whom they pay the yearly Government tax or tribute to the local Khyoungtha Chiefs, whose supremacy they recognize. The wildest clan among them is the Reeang. Indeed, it is only of late years that this clan has settled down peaceably within British territory. Their villages formerly were far away in the Kookie country, and they took part with the independent tribes in the savage raids on British subjects, the perpetration of which led to the direct administration of the Hill Tracts by our Government. Since they have seen that a stable executive authority has been established in the hills, the villages have one by one left the Kookie country, and moved to within the sphere of the British authority.

The chief men among the Tipperahs in this district are Kisto Chunder Thakoor and his brother Modho Chunder, who live in the country bordering on the Fenny River. They are near relatives of the present Rajah of Hill Tipperah, and in 1860 seemed to think that they had some claim to succeed to the Raj, as at that time, owing to the dissensions between them and the Rājāh, they fled hither, and obtaining the assistance of the Kookies, committed the outrages of 1860, which led to Major Raban's expedition against the independent tribes. The Tipperahs, however, seem to have no tribal or feudal attachment to these brothers; they are feared, but neither respected nor loved by the people of their tribe in the Hill Tracts; and there seems to be no inclination or wish on the part of the people to constitute or recognize them as Chiefs in any way.

The Tipperah customs in these hills are much affected by the locality of their villages. Having, as it were, no distinct and collective nationality, they are apt to fuse with, and amalgamate in, customs at any rate with the races with whom they are brought in contact. Thus the Reeangs differ very little in habitudes from the Kookies. The great Nowuttea clan, with its many sub-divisions, living for the most part in the Mong Rajah's country, on the banks of the Fenny, are in close contact with the Bengallees of the plains. They are consequently addicted to Hindoo superstitions and observances, and I regret to say that latterly there have been some slight indications that the most important men among them are fostering the hurtful and obnoxious doctrine of caste and niceties of feeding. Again, the Osuies will be found, most of them, able to talk the Arracanese vernacular, and with ideas assimilating to those of the Khyoungtha.

When a Tipperah dies his body is immediately removed from within the house to the open air. A fowl is killed and placed with some rice at the dead man's feet. The body is burnt at the water side. At the spot where the body was first laid out, the deceased's relatives kill a cock every morning for seven days, and leave it there with some rice as an offering to the manes of the dead. A month after death a like offering is made at the place of cremation, and this is occasionally repeated for a year. The ashes are deposited on a hill in a small hut built for the purpose, in which are also placed the dead man's weapons,—a spear, dâos of two sorts (one his fighting dâo, the other his every-day bread-winner), arrow heads, his metal-stemmed pipe, earrings, and ornaments. The place is held sacred. In all ceremonies of a religious nature among them the "ojha," or "owkchye," is in much request. The ojha is simply an exorcist, or person supposed to have power over spirits; the office depends upon a knowledge of charms, and is therefore necessarily handed down from father to son.

The classification of the Tipperahs, as belonging to the Toungtha, is perhaps incorrect, as in many of their habits and customs they assimilate both with the Bengallees of the plains and with the Khyoungtha tribes; and they possess, also, a distinct head or Chief in the adjacent district of Hill Tipperah, who is recognized as Rajah by the whole race. I have, however, so classed them, as I believe that they belong to the same branch. Among the wilder clans, the Reeangs for instance, they still live in accordance with primitive customs; and in Hill Tipperah the Rankhul and Dhopa clans are called Kookies, but, as far as habits of life and customs go, are much the same as the Reeangs. As I have before said, however, the Tipperah, where he is brought into contact with, or under the influence of, the Bengallee, easily acquires their worst vices and superstitions, losing at the same time the leading characteristic of the primitive man—the love of truth. In an account of Arracan by Colonel Sir A. P. Phayre, which appeared in the Bengal Asiatic Society's Journal, it is said that a people, called Mroongs by the Arracanese, are found in the Akyab District. They announce themselves as descendants of persons carried away from Tipperah several generations back by the Arracan Kings, by whom they were first planted on the Lé-myo River, with a view to cutting off their retreat into their own country; but when Arracan became convulsed in consequence of the invasion of the Burmese, they gradually commenced leaving the Lé-myo, and returning through the hills to their own country. For a time they dwelt on the Koladyne; but none are now to be found in Arracan, save on the Mayoo on its upper course, and only a few stragglers there. The language of the

Mroongs is identical with the Tipperah tongue. The Mroongs referred to by him are still living in the southern part of this district; their villages are principally situated in the valley of the Matamoree River and its tributaries. Their customs and habits differ in no essential particular from those of the rest of the Tipperah clans.

The whole Tipperah tribe is known to the Khyoungtha by the name of Mroong. I have visited some of the Mroong villages on the Matamoree River. They are very hospitable, and I was perforce compelled to go from house to house; in every dwelling a fresh pot of "seepah" being broached. They have a most curious musical instrument, in sound something between an organ and a bagpipe. It is made from a gourd, into which long reedpipes of different lengths are inserted, which have each one hole-stop; this is their sole instrument. Towards the close of the day, becoming enthusiastic, they performed a dance for me, and the instruments which accompanied the measure were single reeds, each player having one reed on which he played his solitary note as his turn came round, after the manner of the old-fashioned Russian horn bands. The tune was monotonous, but not inharmonious. Little boys played the tenor reeds, and men the bass, while every now and then a gong would sound a deep sonorous note that chimed in with the melody in a quaint barbaric manner.

Men only took part in the dance, the women being shy before a stranger. The dancers stood in a circle, turning now to the right and again to the left in unison and at certain periods in the rhythm of the music. The music was as it were punctuated by the dancers bending their knees, and at the end of the movement came a sharp jerky pause. It is curious to compare this dance with a description of a like performance which Baron Humboldt describes in his travels[8].

[8] "The travellers saw the Indians dance. The men, young and old, formed a circle holding each other's hands, and turned sometimes to the right and sometimes

While they were playing, a tame "beemraj" (a small bird) came and settled on the turban of the Roaja, or village head man, and fluttered its wings in apparent delight at the noise. The little children had tame lizards in a string for playthings.

The Tipperahs have a separate and distinct language of their own, but they have no written character.

An account of the tribe as it exists in Hill Tipperah, will be found in the Annual Report to the Surveyor-General for 1863-64 of Mr. R. B. Smart, of the Revenue Survey. He appends to the report a vocabulary of the Tipperah tongue. He has, however, been misled, as the words given by him are not the Tipperah language, but a dialect of the

to the left for whole hours with silent gravity. Feeble sounds, drawn from a series of reeds of different lengths, formed a slow and plaintive accompaniment. The first dancer, to mark the time, bent both knees at the cadence. Sometimes they all made a pause in their places, and executed little oscillatory movements, bending the body from one side to the other."—*Voyage aux Regions Equinoxiales du Nouveau Continent.—Humboldt.*

Lhoossai tongue, spoken by the Rankhul Kookies who reside on the borders of Hill Tipperah.

The Kumi, or Kweymee, dwell on the Koladan River in Arracan and on the upper portion of the Sungoo River, or Rigray Khyoung, in the Chittagong Hill Tracts. The name Kweymee is Arracanese, and was applied to this tribe first, I imagine, because it was something like their own tribal name of Kumi, and, secondly, on account of a peculiarity in their dress. "Kwey," or "Khwee," in Arracanese, means a dog, and "mee" is an affix conveying the idea of men; Kweymee therefore means dog-men. Now the Kumi wear a very scanty breech cloth, which is so adjusted, that a long end hangs down behind them in the manner of a tail; add to this that the dog is a favourite article of food among them, and the derivation of the name seems pretty clear. Colonel Sir A. P. Phayre, in his paper on the Indo-Chinese Borderers, published in the Journal of the Asiatic Society of Bengal (No. 1 of

1853), says that the Kumi have lived on the Koladan River only for the last four or five generations. They had expelled the Mrú tribe from that part of the country, and were themselves being driven west and south by more powerful tribes. Mr. Hodgson, in the same number of the Asiatic Society's Journal, states his belief that the Kumi, Khyeng, and Mrú are aboriginal inhabitants of the country, broken and dispersed into different tribes. In the Chittagong Hills the Kumi tribe numbers some 2000 souls. Their numbers, however, fluctuate, as year by year some families either go to, or return from, their relatives living on the Koladan in Arracan. The journey is always made by a well-known pass across the hills, leading from the Sungoo River over Modho Tong. The distance is a short two days' journey. The Pee Khyoung in Arracan is reached on the first day.

The Kumis pay three rupees per house yearly to the Bohmong, whom they recognize as their ruler.

In common with all hill tribes, each village has its recognized head, who receives no money tribute, but has certain definite rights and privileges pertaining to his position. The Kumis, owing to their more immediate juxtaposition with the independent and predatory tribes, are more warlike than the majority of our hill dwellers. Their villages are generally situated on the top of a lofty hill, and are regularly stockaded and fortified. The village has generally but one door, and this is defended by a winding passage trebly stockaded. The door itself is of solid timber, thickly studded from top to bottom with a thicket of bamboo spikes. The *enceinte* of the village has lofty look-out stations placed at intervals, where a watch is kept day and night; the steep slopes of the hill are rendered difficult of ascent by *chevaux de frise* of bamboo, while the ravines below are strewn with caltrops. In one village I noticed a most extraordinary stronghold in a tree. It was a small house built of shot-proof logs of timber, and elevated about 100 feet from the ground in the branches of an enormous tree that grew in the village. The hut was capable of holding about twenty persons; it was loopholed all round and in the floor, and was reached by a ladder which could be drawn up when necessary. It was probably some such structure as this that led to the tale of the tree-living Kookies which Colonel Phayre notices. (Journal of Bengal Asiatic Society for 1841.) Certain it is that none of the tribes known to us live in trees, although it is not improbable that some such device as that described above might be resorted to by them as a safeguard and retreat in the event of a night attack or a surprise.

The Kumi houses are all built of bamboo and thatched with palm-shaped leaves, which are found in moist places in the jungle. The houses are always raised 8 or 10 feet from the ground. There is a platform in front of the house where the plates and dishes are washed, and where the bamboo tubes, in which the women fetch water, are kept. The house itself consists of one immense hall with an enclosed platform at the back. This hall is about 50 feet long by 20 broad; it has two large fire-places, or hearths, one at each end, made in the usual way of loose earth battened into a square between four logs. The walls are double, of bamboo mat, with about 18 inches between the outer and inner wall; this, no doubt, adds greatly to the coolness of the house, but must prevent the free incoming of the breeze. Outside the house, along the whole plinth above the door, is a line of skulls, antlered deer, and tusked boar, guyal and bear, all smoked to one uniform dark brown tinge. Inside the house, towards the centre, if the owner is a mighty hunter, will be seen another trophy of arms and skins, including buffaloo horns, and mixed with weapons, such as shields, powder horns, spears, &c. Guns (if there be any) are generally kept concealed.

The Kumis have a tradition of the Creation, but I am unable to say whether it is peculiar to them or derived from some other source. It is as follows:—"God made the world and the trees and the creeping things first, and after that he set to work to make one man and one woman, forming their bodies of clay; but each night, on the completion of his work, there came a great snake, which, while God was sleeping, devoured the two images. This happened twice or thrice, and God was at his wit's end, for he had to work all day, and could not finish the pair in less than twelve hours; besides, if he did not sleep, he would be no good," said my informant. "If he were not obliged to sleep, there would be no death, nor would mankind be afflicted with illness. It is when he rests that the snake carries us off to this day. Well, he was at his wit's end, so at last he got up early one morning and first made a dog and put life into it, and that night, when he had finished the images, he set the dog to watch them, and when the snake came, the dog barked and frightened it away. This is the reason at this day that when a man is dying the dogs begin to howl; but I suppose God sleeps heavily now-a-days, or the snake is bolder, for men die all the same."

When small-pox first made its appearance among the Kumis, they considered it to be a devil that had come from Arracan. The villages were put in "khang," and all egress or ingress put a stop to. A monkey was killed by dashing it on the ground, and was then suspended at the village gate; a mixture of monkey's blood and small river pebbles was sprinkled on the houses, and the threshold of each house swept with the monkey's tail, and the fiend was adjured to depart; but the poor Kumis found that this was a very strong devil indeed, for the exorcisms were of no effect. They therefore abandoned their homes, leaving the sick to take care of themselves; and men, women, and children, fled to the jungles.

Kumi music is made with a sort of guitar, in shape not unlike a large fiddle, but made of one solid lump of wood, with wooden frets tied down the stem, as in a guitar. It is thrummed with a bit of bamboo; drums of every size give an *ad libitum* accompaniment. Their dance is simple. It is more a species of march than a dance: about twenty young men move round in a circle to measured time; the rhythm distinctly marked, both by the music and by the motions of the dancers. The leader, on the occasion I saw them dance, held in his hand a small dâo with a brazen handle, from which streamed a tuft of goats' hair dyed scarlet. The other performers bore, some a shield, some an ordinary dâo or a spear; and these weapons they clanked together in time to their movements. The measure went something in this fashion:—One step, a pause; two steps, all sink down on their hams, clank weapons, and rise again; another step, then a jump and a shout, and so on. In an adjoining room to that in which this dance took place were the drinkers, two to each pot of "seepah," which they sucked vigorously through reeds.

The religion of the Kumis is the same as that of the other Toungtha tribes. They offer sacrifice to the spirits of the hills and rivers. On one occasion I had to swear an oath of friendship with certain Chiefs among the Kumis, and sacrifice was then offered up as follows:—A goat was tied by the neck, the cord being held by me; another rope was fastened to the animal's hind legs, and held by the five Chiefs with whom I was concerned. The ropes were kept taut, so that the animal was thrown into an extended position. The head Chief bearing a fighting dâo, stood over the goat; and taking a mouthful of liquor from a cup which was handed to him, he blew it first over me, then over the Chiefs, and a third mouthful upon the goat. He then raised his dâo over his head, and addressed a loud invocation to the "Nat," or spirit of the river, at the same time plucking some hairs from the goat, and scattering them to the wind. Then with one stroke of the dâo he severed the animal's head from its body. The warm blood from his weapon was afterwards smeared upon the feet and foreheads of all who took part in the ceremony, with a muttered formula, indicating that any one who was false or acted contrary to the object for the attainment of which the sacrifice was offered, could be slain without fault by his coadjutors. A grand feast on the goat's flesh concluded the ceremony.

The marrying of a wife among them does not appear to entail the performance of any particular ceremonies. It is simply a festive occasion, when much is eaten and drunk. The practice of taking the omens from certain conditions of a fowl's tongue seems to prevail among them as among the Khyoungtha. A child is named on the falling off of the navel string. In giving it a name, the mother binds seven threads round its wrist, saying, "Be fortunate! be brave! be healthy!" The name given is generally one that has been borne by some progenitor. They have no special festival days; a fortunate war-party, a marriage, or a lucky hunt, are all occasions for merry-making. They are large drinkers, and they smoke tobacco freely, either from a bamboo pipe, or rolled up as a cigar. A favourite festival dish among them is a dog stuffed with rice. The young cur is plentifully fed with cooked rice about half an hour before cooking time, and when stuffed to repletion is knocked on the head, skinned and roasted. The rice is left in the stomach and eaten with the dog's flesh as a concomitant relish. Surely men's appetites and their wits are sharpened on the same grindstone.

Women among them have no rights of inheritance; the eldest son is recognized as his father's sole heir and representative. Slavery is a recognized institution among them. They burn their dead, first filling the mouth of the corpse with rice and rice beer. The ashes are afterwards placed in a small hut built near the place of cremation. Here are also deposited the every-day clothes, the eating utensils, and the sleeping mat of the deceased. They have no salutations or forms of greeting among them; neither does their language contain any precative terms: they have no written character.

The Kumis wear their hair bound in a knot over their foreheads. Their earrings are flat discs of silver, with the centre cut out; among the women the lobe of the ear is distended to a large size, with a roll of cloth or a flattened cylinder of wood.

The Mrú tribe formerly dwelt in the Arracan Hills; they now live principally to the west of the River Sungoo, and on the Matamoree River in this district. They state that they were driven from Arracan by the Kumi tribe, between whom and themselves, within the last few years, a blood feud existed, and affrays often took place. The spread of British influence among both tribes has now put a stop to these encounters. The Rajaweng, or History of Arracan, states that a Mrú was King of Arracan in the 14th century A.D. The Mrús are despised as wild men by the Khyoungtha: they are tributary to the Bohmong, a Chief of Arracanese stock, residing at Bundrabun, on the Sungoo River. They are perhaps the weakest tribe in the hills, not numbering more than 1500 souls.

They have no written language. In physique they are tall, powerful men, dark-complexioned, but with no traces of the Mongol in their faces. They have no medicine among them. To sores or wounds they apply a poultice of pounded rice or the earth of an ant-hill made into mud with warm water. Headaches are cured by biting the head till the blood flows. In cases of colic, a favourite remedy is a hot dâo applied to the stomach over a wet cloth. They are subject to fevers and inflammation of the bowels from over-drinking. They are a peaceable people, timid and simple. In a dispute they do not fight, but call in an "ojha," or exorcist, who takes the sense of the spirits in the matter. In taking a journey, on starting in the morning, each man takes a young green shoot of "sunn" grass, and the leading man, going ankle-deep into the stream, offers up a prayer to the water kelpie, the others standing meanwhile reverently on the marge. The shoots are then planted in the sand along the edge of the stream; also, on crossing a hill, each man, on reaching the crest, plucks a fresh young shoot of grass, and places it on a pile of the withered offerings of former journeyers who have gone before. They have three gods, viz.: Túrai, the great All-father; Sung-túng, the hill spirit; and Oreng, the deity of the rivers. Their ideas as to a future state are formless; their oath is by gun, dâo, and the tiger. On solemn occasions they will swear by one of their gods, to whom, at the same time, a sacrifice must be offered; the breaking of an oath of this description is sure to be punished by disease, ill luck, and death. They have no recollection of there having been at any time any great chief or ruler memorable in the tribe: they have always, they say, been a wandering and a scattered people. Before marriage the sexes have unrestrained intercourse. In naming a child, three or four names are fixed upon, and they determine which it shall be by the throwing of cowries; when all the shells turn in one way upwards, that name is chosen. The child is named one day after birth.

A young man has to serve three years for his wife in his father-in-law's house; or, if he be wealthy, he can dispense with this preliminary by paying 200 or 300 rupees down. At the marriage there is, of course, a big feast and a corresponding drink. Every one attending a marriage has a thread tied round his right wrist; this is done by the oldest woman of the bride's family. This string must remain on the wrist until it drops off by wear and tear, the wearer must not remove the string himself; it is called the "bom-gom." Their favourite time for dancing is a moonlight night. They use the same kind of reedpipes as the Mroongs. The boys play at "konyon," or, as they call the game, "tsing khing;" and the peg-top is also a favourite plaything. Their earrings and ornaments are the same as those worn by the Kumi.

On a man dying and leaving a young family, his eldest and nearest adult male relative takes the family and the deceased's wife to live with him. If a man has sons and daughters, and they marry, he will live with his youngest child, who also inherits all property on the death of the father. The villagers choose their own head man, but a Roaja's son generally succeeds to his father's place. In cases of divorce the husband is repaid all that he gave for his wife, and she has to leave behind her all her ornaments. A widow may marry again, but a second marriage is unusual among women. Slavery is an ancient institution among them. Two sorts of slavery are recognized: captives taken in war and debtor slaves. Both are treated alike. The master of a female slave cannot marry or have connexion with her. Any other person can do so by paying her price, and so making her free. All children are free. Concubinage is unknown among the Mrú. They drink milk and eat the flesh of the cow, or indeed any kind of flesh. All the Hill races indeed may be broadly distinguished as flesh-eaters from those of the plains, whose ordinary diet is farinaceous. This principle of diet may, I think, be largely accountable for the superiority in character possessed by the men of the hills over the plain dwellers. Rousseau says, "Il est certain que les grands mangeurs de viande sont en general cruels et feroces plus que les autres hommes" (Emile, vol. i. p. 274). Sir William Temple also, in his account of the United Provinces, remarks that all fierce and bold animals are carnivorous.

The site of a village is fixed by the dreaming of dreams. If in a dream they see fish, it is good, and they will get money; if they dream of a river, it is also fortunate, as it foretokens a plentiful crop of rice; but if they see a dog or a snake, the site is an unlucky one, and the village ought not to be built there. On the village being built, a big sacrifice is offered to all the gods, and the village is placed in "khang" for three days. When the rice springs up in July, the village is again placed in quarantine; but sacrifice then is only offered to Sung-túng, the god of the hills. They weave their own clothes from cotton grown in their jooms. Their clothing is of the scantiest sort, the men wearing merely one strip of cloth round the waist and between the legs, while the women wear a short petticoat, and have their bosoms completely bare. They seem to think that the tribe is dying out: there are now many more diseases known to them than there used to be in former times; and they say that in their fathers' times men used to live to the age of 100 years, but that now the average duration of life does not exceed fifty or sixty years. The Mrú bury their dead.

The Khyengs, or Khyang, are very few in number in this district; they chiefly inhabit the spurs of the great hill range separating the Hill Tracts from Arracan. They are the offshoots of a large and powerful hill tribe in Burmah, who are as yet said to be independent. In religion and customs they differ in no material particular from the Mrú tribe already described.

These tribes state themselves to be of common origin, sprung from two brothers; and the great similarity in their customs, habits, and language, confirms this statement.

Their account of the creation of man and their origin is characteristic. I give it as nearly as possible in the same words that it was told to me:—

"Formerly our ancestors came out of a cave in the earth, and we had one great Chief, named Tlandrok-pah. He it was who first domesticated the guyal; he was so powerful that he married God's daughter. There were great festivities at the marriage, and Tlandrok-pah made God a present of a famous gun that he had. You can still hear the gun; the thunder is the sound of it. At the marriage, our Chief called all the animals to help to cut a road through the jungle, to God's house, and they all gladly gave assistance to bring home the bride—all save the sloth (the húlúq monkey is his grandson) and the earth-worm; and on this account they were cursed, and cannot look on the sun without dying. The cave whence man first came out is in the Lhoosai country close to

Vanhuilen's village, of the Burdaiya tribe; it can be seen to this day, but no one can enter. If one listens outside, the deep notes of the gong and the sound of men's voices can still be heard. Some time after Tlandrok-pah's marriage, all the country became on fire, and God's daughter told us to come down to the sea-coast, where it is cool; that was how we first came into this country. At that time mankind and the birds and beasts all spoke one language. Then God's daughter complained to her father that her tribe were unable to kill the animals for food, as they talked and begged for life with pitiful words, making the hearts of men soft, so that they could not slay them. On this, God took from the beasts and birds the power of speech, and food became plentiful among us. We eat every living thing that cannot speak. At that time, also, when the great fire broke from the earth, the world became all dark, and men broke up and scattered into clans and tribes. Their languages also became different.

"We have two gods:—Patyen; he is the

greatest: it was he made the world. He lives in the west, and takes charge of the sun at night. Our other god is named Khozing; he is the patron of our tribe, and we are specially loved by him. The tiger is Khozing's house-dog, and he will not hurt us, because we are the children of his master."

The great distinction between the Pankho and Bunjogee tribes is the mode of wearing the hair. The Pankhos bind their hair in a knot at the back of the head in the same way as the Tipperahs and Lhoosai do; but the Bunjogees, like the Shendus and Kumi tribe, tie up their hair in a knot on the top of the head over the forehead. As it is considered a beauty to have long, thick hair, the young men of the Bunjogees stuff a large ball of black cotton into their topknot to make it look bigger. The origin of the mode in which the Bunjogees wear their hair is as follows:—One day the squirrel and the horned owl had a quarrel, and the squirrel bit the owl on his head, so that he became all bloody; and when the squirrel saw the owl under this new aspect, he became frightened and ran away, and the owl devoured all his young ones. A Bunjogee Chief observed this; he was a "Koa-vang," and the tiger came and told him that what he had seen was a message from Khozing. Thus it is that when the Bunjogees go to war, they bind their hair over the forehead, and put red cloth in their hair, so that like the horned owl they may take heads.

The two tribes are not numerically strong: they number about 700 houses or 3000 souls. There are three villages of Pankhos, and one of Bunjogees living in the country bordering on the Kurnafoolee; the majority, however, are found in the Bohmong's country to the east of the Sungoo River. Their language strongly resembles that of the Lhoosai; and in physique and appearance also one would suppose them to be an offshoot of that tribe. They, however, affirm that they came originally from the south, and are sprung from the great nation of Shans in Burmah. Some of their customs also differ materially from those of the Lhoosai. For instance, the Lhoosai and our Chukmas bind their grain in baskets, while the Pankhos and Bunjogee reap and sheave it. Again, they bury their dead feet northward, but the Lhoosai dry and preserve their dead. In the time of one of their Rajahs, Ngúngjúngnúng, the Pankhos and Bunjogees assert that they were the dominant and most numerous of all the tribes in this part of the world. They attribute the decline of their power to the dying out of the old stock of Chiefs to whom divine descent was attributed. Although admitting the supremacy of one great god, the Pankhos and Bunjogees offer no worship to him; all their reverence and sacrificial rites are directed towards Khozing, the patron deity of their nation. In some villages are men said to be specially marked out as a medium of intercourse between Khozing and his children. Such a possessed person is called "Koavang." He becomes filled with, and possessed by, the divine afflatus. During these moments of inspiration he is said by his fellows to possess the gift of tongues and to be invulnerable. He can also caress tigers unharmed. It is generally a male who is thus gifted: the favour of God falls seldom on the weaker sex. He it is who makes sacrifice and interprets the omens by examination of the entrails. The "Koa-vang" receives no payment or other consideration save the honour accruing to him by his position as interpreter of the wishes and commands of Khozing. The god Khozing has a village somewhere in these hills, where he lives; but no mortal can enter it. Formerly one of the Bunjogee Chiefs was leading a war-party against the Lhoosai, and he came in sight of Khozing's village; it was situated on a very high hill, and hung round with red and white cloth. The Chief wished to surprise this village, and get some heads; for to be the possessor of a large number of human heads is the acmé of Bunjogee happiness. So he went towards the village for ten days, but got no nearer to it, and at last it receded altogether from sight. Then the Chief knew that it was the village of Khozing.

After death they believe that the deceased

go into the large hill whence man first emerged; this they say is the land of the dead: but although they wish to return, and weep much, they are unable to do so if they have led a bad life in this world; but if otherwise, Khozing sometimes sends them back in a new body. Sacrifice is offered inside the house. In former times they used to offer human sacrifices; but although this practice is still considered very beneficial, and great plenty would result from the rite should they do so, they are prevented from the good act by fear of the Government. The great oath is by dâo, spear, gun, and blood: this must be taken by the side of a river; but it is a solemn undertaking, and only to be performed on great occasions. Should a person disregard this oath, he and his family will certainly die a violent death. On ordinary occasions an oath is taken by the Chief's spear; for instance, if any thing were stolen in a village, the spear of the Chief is stuck in the ground at the gate of the village, and every one who passes has to take hold of it and swear that they know nothing of the matter in question. Whoever will not thus swear, has to account for whatever may have been stolen.

In ordinary sacrifices each man is his own priest. On the birth of a child a pig must be sacrificed at the foot of the house ladder, and a fowl on the river bank. When the child is named, which is on the seventh day after birth, a red cock is sacrificed, and five jars of "seepah" drunk if it is a son; while for a daughter, two hens are offered up and three pots of "seepah" are disposed of. If a married woman goes astray, her seducer is not punished, but the woman is fined, and has her ears cut off. The intercourse between both sexes is free and unrestrained until after marriage.

In making a marriage the omens are always carefully consulted, such as the tongue of a fowl, the interior of an egg, &c. To see a deer is a bad omen; a tiger, a good one. Auspicious dreams also are requisite before a marriage can be contracted. They have no festivals in the year, save one at the sprouting of the young rice, and then Patyen, the supreme god, is implored to grant a plentiful harvest. The success of a war-party or the killing of big game in the chase forms occasions for merry-making. In observing quarantine they follow the same ceremonies as have been previously described as prevalent among the Toungtha. The Bunjogees bury their dead. A Chief is buried in a sitting posture. They are entirely ignorant of medicine. In cases of illness they offer sacrifice to avert the anger of the deity who has sent the disorder. They also use the gall and dung of the boa-constrictor, mixed with spirits, as a universal remedy. In general customs and habits they assimilate closely with the Lhoosai, of whom I shall next proceed to speak.

The Lhoosai, commonly called the Kookies, are a powerful and independent people, who touch upon the borders of the Chittagong Hill Tracts. They extend in numberless hordes, north and north-east, until they reach

Cachar on the one hand, and the frontiers of Burmah on the other. They cannot be considered as a nation, for they have no coherence of government or policy, but, with slight differences, they speak one language and follow the same customs. They are known to the Bengallees by the name of Kookie, and to the Burmese as the Lankhé[9]. Our knowledge of the Lhoosai clans is of course confined to the tribes on our immediate frontier, with whom we have been brought into contact. They are three in number, viz., the Howlong, the Syloo, and the Rutton Poiya clans. Their numbers were estimated as follow by Captain Graham in 1861:—

Howlong	12,600
Syloo	10,800
Rutton Poiya . . .	2,580

In comparing the Lhoosai dialect with the hill languages given by Major MacCulloch in

[9] The people of Bhootan, who are of undoubted Thibetan origin, call themselves Lhotsa. Can this bear any affinity to "Lhoosai"?

his account of Munnipoor, published by the Government of India, although many words are found to be identical, and the derivation of the tribes from a common stock seems certain, yet the Lhoosai dialect is substantially different from those of the Munnipooree hill tribes given by MacCulloch. It would seem of closest affinity to those of the Murring and Thada Kookies of the Munnipoor frontier. Mr. Hunter, in his Rural Annals of Bengal, p. 144, states, "In the district between Kamaun and Assam, one inquirer counted 28 distinct dialects mutually unintelligible to the different tribes who use them. Among the Naga tribes, also, about 30 languages exist, affording a striking proof of the tendency of unwritten language to split up into dialects." Captain Stewart, also, in his account of the hill tribes of Cachar, concurs in this idea. I must needs add that my experience somewhat militates against this theory. I have found the Lhoosai language almost identical with the tongue of the Pankho and Bunjogee tribes. The different tribes of Lhoosai also on our frontier speak (with slight differences) the same dialect; and this, too, in spite of all these tribes being widely scattered apart over the country, and in many cases having no intercourse with each other. Note, moreover, that the Tipperah tongue is spoken in the same manner and understood by all the numerous clans of that tribe both in this district and in Hill Tipperah. The Mrúngs, also, originally from Tipperah, who have no intercourse with their parent tribe, nor have seen their native country for more than 150 years, still preserve their vernacular unchanged to any material extent. There is certainly not so much difference as there is between the English tongue as commonly spoken, and the blurred *patois* of a Somersetshire labourer.

The theory in question, therefore, appears to me to deserve more close and careful investigation before a decisive conclusion can be arrived at.

Besides the three large Lhoosai clans with which we are well acquainted, there exist many more, known to us by hearsay. The village system among the Kookies is best described as a series of petty states, each under a Dictator or President. To illustrate the position of the Chief, or President, I may mention that in 1866, when on a visit to the village of one of the leading Chiefs among the Lhoosai, I was standing talking with him in the path that ran through the village. While we were thus standing a drunken Lhoosai came stumbling along, and finding us somewhat in the way, he seized the Chief by the neck and shoved him off the path, asking why he stopped the road. On my asking the Chief for an explanation of such disrespect being permitted, he replied, "On the war-path or in the council I am Chief, and my words are obeyed; behaviour like that would be punished by death. Here, in the village, that drunkard is my fellow and equal." In like manner any presents given to the Chief are common property. His people walk off with them, saying, "He is a big man, and will get lots more given to him. Who will give to us if he does not?" On the other hand, all that is in his village belongs to the Chief; he can and does call upon people to furnish him with everything that he requires. A Chief's son, on attaining manhood, does not, as a rule, remain with his father; he sets up a separate village of his own. The men of one Chief can transfer their allegiance to another at will; hence it happens that a Chief's village becomes large or small as he is successful in war, or the reverse. Chiefship, however, is confined to a certain clan called "Aidey," from whence all the tribes are said originally to have sprung. Only the son of a Chief can set up a village for himself. Hence there is a fiction that all Chiefs are blood-relatives, and it is consequently forbidden to kill a Chief, or, as he is called, Lal, save in the heat of battle. The Lal directs in war; he is the last in the advance, and the rearmost in retreat.

The house of a Lal is a harbour of refuge. A criminal or fugitive taking shelter there cannot be harmed; but he becomes the slave of the Lal, under whose protection he has placed himself. Each man is bound to labour three days yearly for his Chief, and each house in the village furnishes its share of any expense incurred in feeding or entertaining the Lal's guests. The Chief's house also is built for him by the voluntary labour of his people. The residence of a powerful Chief is generally surrounded by the houses of his slaves, who marry and cultivate, enjoying undisturbed the fruits of their labour. On the death of a slave, however, his wife and children and all his property go to the Chief. The messages and errands of a Lal, or Chief, are done by his favourite slaves. They are his ambassadors in war.

To collect his people, or in fact to authenticate any order, the Chief's spear, which is usually carved and ornamented, is sent by a messenger from village to village. Should the message be a hostile one, the messenger carries a fighting dâo, to which a piece of red cloth is attached. Another method is by the "phuroi," which is a species of wand made out of strips of peeled bamboo, about eight inches long, in this shape (†). If the tips of the cross-pieces be broken, a demand for black mail is indicated; a rupee to be levied for each break. If the end of one of the cross-pieces is charred it implies urgency, and that the people are to come even by torch-light. If a capsicum be fixed on to the "phuroi," it signifies that disobedience to the order will meet with punishment as severe as the capsicum is hot. If the cross-piece is of cane, it means that disobedience will entail corporal punishment. Among the Lhoosai, women cannot inherit. Property is divided amongst the sons; the youngest, however, gets the largest share; the rest in equal portions. Widows can marry again, but do not often avail themselves of the privilege if they have children, as a widowed mother is paramount in a son's house.

They have no caste or class distinctions among them; all eat and drink together, and one man is as good as another. Marriage is a civil contract, soluble at the will of both parties concerned. A woman, on leaving her husband, takes with her only what she brought originally from her father's house. There are no sacrifices or other religious ceremonies on the occasion of a marriage—only a big feast and a dance. Adultery is very uncommon. It is punished by the death of both parties; a husband is allowed to cut them down, and no fault attaches to him; their only shelter is in the Chief's house and a life-long slavery. Concubinage, or whoredom, is unknown among the Lhoosai; but the intercourse between the unmarried of both sexes is entirely unchecked—a girl may go with any young man she fancies. If parents marry a girl to a man whom she does not like, she generally runs away from her husband, and is not thought to be wrong in doing so.

Women are generally held in consideration among the Lhoosai; their advice is taken, and they have much influence. Should the father of a house die, his wife becomes the head of the family. Upon the women, however, falls the whole burden of the bodily labour by which life is supported. They fetch water, hew wood, cultivate and help to reap the crop, besides spinning, cooking, and brewing. The men employ themselves chiefly in making forays upon weaker tribes, or in hunting. Of home work, they only clear the ground and help to carry the harvest; they also build the house. The men are generally to be seen lounging about, cleaning their arms, drinking, or smoking. A strange custom exists among them, that when a man, either through laziness, cowardice, or bodily incapacity, is unable to do his work, he is dressed in women's clothes, and consorts and works with the women. I have seen instances of this in several villages. The Lhoosai, as a rule, are not prolific; a family is generally limited to three or four children. A child is suckled for a great length of time. They sometimes do not leave the breast until four years old.

Crime is rare among them. Theft in a man's own village is unknown, but they will sometimes steal if visiting another clan. On such a theft being discovered, the Chief, in whose village it has been committed, sends and makes a formal complaint to the Chief under whom the thief is living. The goods stolen are, if discovered, given up, and the offender is fined. Should a man be fined so heavily that he is unable to pay, he becomes the slave of his Chief. A life is exacted for a life. The murderer will not escape, even by taking refuge in the Chief's house; the relatives will cut him down. If, however, the Chief's wife adopts him as a son, he escapes scatheless. No vendettas, or blood-feuds, are carried on among them. They reverence parents, and honour old age. When past work, the father and mother are supported by their children. They have no salutation or greetings among them, nor does their language contain any precative affixes or expressions.

The religion of the Lhoosai and their traditions as to origin are similar to those already described of the Pankho tribe.

In physique both men and women are well-made and wonderfully muscular. The average height of the males is about 5 feet 8 inches, and of the women 5 feet 4 inches. They are never corpulent. Their physiognomy is not pleasing, being generally of a sulky and forbidding appearance. They differ entirely from the other hill tribes of Burman or Arracanese origin, in that their faces bear no marks of Tartar or Mongolian descent. They are swarthy in complexion, and their cheeks are generally smooth among the Howlong tribe. However, one meets many men having long, bushy beards. I should be inclined to attribute this to a mixture of Bengallee blood, from the many captives they have from time to time carried away; but I have seen old men white-bearded, and we possess no record of any Lhoosai raids so long as even thirty or forty years ago.

The men wear one long home-spun sheet or mantle of cotton cloth, and, save this, they have no other garment. These mantles are sometimes of very good manufacture; the best description are dyed blue and interwoven with crimson and yellow stripes. They are fond of wearing in the ear a small bunch of brilliant feathers. Their hair is bound into a knot on the nape of the neck. The women wear a strip of thick blue cloth round the loins, about eighteen inches in breadth; their bosoms being left bare. They distend the lobe of the ear to an enormous size with circular discs of wood or ivory. Both sexes attach the greatest value to amber, which is worn in large cylindrical beads as a necklace. They attach a fabulous value to some of these necklaces. The amber is said to be brought from Burmah.

A Lhoosai village is always situated on the top of a high hill, and in time of war is fortified by a stockade of heavy timber logs. The time that a village stays in one place is determined by the facilities afforded for cultivation in the neighbourhood. When all the land within easy reach is exhausted, the village is moved to a fresh site. The ordinary time of remaining in one place is four to five years. The houses are built, not of bamboos, as is usual in the hills, but of logs, and thatched with the palmated leaf commonly used throughout the hills for that purpose. At the door of every house is a small raised platform, where, in the cool of the evening, the men lounge about and whittle sticks. The interior of most houses is partitioned off into sleeping and living rooms. The houses are low-pitched, and the floor is raised from the ground some four feet. A Chief's house is simply an enlarged edition of the ordinary Lhoosai house. In a Chief's house at all times one is sure to find two or three men imbibing "khong" out of horn cups. Among the other tribes "khong" and "seepah" are sucked up through a long reed out of the jar, as we drink sherry-cobbler; but among the Lhoosai they empty the jars (which are full of rice, water, and the other things from which the liquor is brewed) by means of a syphon made from two pieces of reed joined together by lac or resin at an angle of about 45°. In the Chief's house will be seen also large brazen vessels, embossed with Burmese characters, for containing rice, and the big gong which tolls out when the council of war is assembled, or when the Chief calls his people together. On one occasion my predecessor, Captain Graham, was visiting a Kookie village, and he discovered that they held some British subjects in captivity. On demanding their release, however, the Chief refused to let them go; and Captain Graham equally refusing to go without them, things began to look mischievous. At length the Chief in a rage betook himself off to his house, and the big gong began to toll. Captain Graham describes the effect as miraculous: every woman and child disappeared from sight as if by magic, and the Lhoosai, with their weapons in their hands, came crowding to the Chief. Matters, however, were eventually arranged on a peaceable footing, and the captives were released.

Two animals domesticised among the Lhoosai strike one immediately on entering a village; they are the guyal and the hill goat. Nearly every house has its guyal tethered near the door; they are not fed in the village, but simply receive salt, of which they are immoderately fond, at their owner's hand. Early at the first dim break of dawn, they troop out of the village to pasture, untended by any cattle-herd, returning again at night of their own accord. The Kookies do not milk them; they are used only for slaughter at big feasts or sacrifices. In appearance they are magnificent beasts, resembling nothing so much as the Chillingworth wild cattle magnified.[1] The goats

[1] "The guyal delights to range about in the thickest forest, where he browses evening and morning on the tender shoots and leaves of different shrubs, seldom feeding on grass when he can get them. His disposition is gentle; even when wild in his native hills, he is not considered dangerous, never standing the approach of man, and much less bearing his attack. The Kookies hunt the wild ones for the sake of their flesh. Guyals have been domesticated among the Kookies from time immemorial, and without any variation in their appearance from the wild stock. No difference whatever is observed in the appearance of the wild and tame animals, brown of various shades being the general colour of both. The

are remarkable for being pure white, with a long shaggy coat which, in the males, almost

wild guyal is about the size of the wild buffalo in India. The tame guyal among the Kookies being bred in nearly the same habits of freedom and on the same food, without ever undergoing any labour, grows to the same size as the wild one. This animal lives to the age of fifteen or twenty years; and in the fourth year the cows produce, after eleven months' gestation, bearing a calf only once in three years, and so long an interval between each birth must tend to keep the species rare. The calf sucks for eight or nine months, when it is capable of supporting itself. The Kookies tie up the calf until it is of sufficient age to do so. The guyal (cow) gives very little milk, and does not yield it long, but what she gives is of remarkably rich quality, about equally so with the cream of other milk, which it resembles in colour. The Kookies make no use whatever of the milk, but rear their guyals entirely for the sake of their flesh and skins. They make their shields of the hide of this animal. The flesh of the guyal is in the highest estimation among the Kookies; so much so, that no solemn festival is ever celebrated without slaughtering one or more of these beasts, according to the importance of the occasion. The Kookies train their guyals to no labour. The domesticated guyals are allowed by the Kookies to roam at large during the day through the forest in the neighbourhood of the village; but, as evening approaches, they all return home of their own accord, the young sweeps the ground. Of these goats' skins some of the Lhoosai clans make a kind of pouch, with the long hair pendent; this is worn like a Highland sporran. In almost every house will be found a pet pig. This animal goes loose, and is generally enormously fat, having the run of all the leavings in the way of food. Somewhere near the village one is sure to come upon some of their traps for game. They have three kinds of traps:—two for deer and pigs, in which the main-spring is a bent-down sapling, or a strong

guyal being early taught this habit by being regularly fed every night with salt, of which he is very fond; and from the occasional continuance of this practice, as he grows up, the attachment of the guyal to his village becomes so strong, that when the Kookies migrate from it, they are obliged to set fire to their huts lest their guyal should return thither from their new place of residence before they have become equally attached to it as to the former, through the same means. The Kookies give no grain to their cattle. The cry of the guyal has no resemblance to the grunt of the Indian ox, but a good deal resembles that of the buffalo. It is a kind of lowing, but shriller."—*Wild Types and Sources of Domestic Animals, Land and Water*, May 11th, 1867.

bamboo, and which either transfixes the game with an arrow or jerks it high and pendent in the air; the other, generally used for tigers, bears, and such-like game, is a rough cage of logs open at two ends, and placed in the run of the animals whose destruction it is wished to effect. The top of the cage is composed of two or three enormous tree-trunks, so arranged as to fall on and kill any animal attempting to pass through the trap. The Lhoosai are great eaters of flesh, and domestic animals not being very plentiful among them, their supplies depend a good deal upon their success in the chase. They make large hunting parties, and their favourite game is the wild elephant, which abounds throughout the hills. As, however, they are very careless and reckless in the management of their guns and ammunition, a large hunting party seldom returns without one or more of its members having been accidentally shot. It is only within the last ten or twenty years that the Lhoosai have learnt the use of fire-arms; but muskets, mostly of English make and Tower-marked, are now common enough among them, and render what was formerly a horde of simple savages a band of very dangerous marauders. They are constantly warring among themselves; or when a short interval of comparative peace comes, they make a raid upon the nearest British territory to procure slaves. Lately, however, the leading Chiefs among the Lhoosai have sworn a solemn and lasting peace with the British authorities. The whole art of war among them may be described in one word—surprise. They never advance openly to attack an enemy, but send forward spies to make sure of taking their foe unawares. Should their object be discovered, they at once abandon the attack, and retreat as they came. A sacrifice and a big drink is always an indispensable preliminary to an expedition.

On starting for a raid, the old men and women of the village accompany the party an hour's journey on their way, carrying the provisions, and then leave them with loud wishes for their success. "May you be unhurt, and bring home many heads," is the formula. This is when open hostilities have commenced with some other clan; but if a virgin enterprise is to be inaugurated, it is a *sine quâ non* among them that no woman should know a word about the matter. They will march four and five days, traversing enormous distances to the village they intend to attack, and burst upon their prey about an hour before dawn. A young man of the Pankho tribe gave me the following sketch:—"When I was quite a little boy, my father and mother lived in Ardung Roaja's village, and the Lhoosai battle came to us. It was one night when all the village had well drunken. Our village was on a spur of a lofty hill in the valley of the Sungoo. The women used to go down an hour's journey every day to bring water in the bamboo tubes which we use for the purpose. The hill spur at the back of the village was defended by a double palissade, inside which a sentry was always posted; on the other three sides the village was inaccessible. About four in the morning, when it was neither light nor dark, the sentry saw something moving in the jungle outside the stockade, and he thought it was a guyal or a jungle pig, and threw a stone at it; then up sprung the Lhoosai, about 200 men, and gave a low guttural shout, hoarse and deep. All our villagers abandoned their houses, and fled for their lives down a concealed path. My mother took me on her back and ran. The Lhoosai only got two of our people, and they were too drunk to move. They hauled one fellow up, but he only grunted and lay down again; then they prodded him with a spear, and he only grunted the more. So they cut him to pieces as he lay. Then they plundered our village and went away." A young man, a Riang Tipperah, who lives in my house, was formerly a slave of Rutton Poia's (a Lhoosai Chief), and I have heard from him many accounts of raids made by his master. He used to accompany the Chief as the bearer of his weapons. His first raid was in 1860, made on the Bengallee inhabitants of Kundal in Tipperah. They fell upon the villagers at day-dawn, according to custom; and the Bengallee men, with one consent, ran away. The women, however, stood their ground, and abused their grim assailants vociferously for breaking into honest people's houses. The Lhoosai laughed at their shrill tongues at first, but later it was found troublesome, and one young woman had to be cut down *pour encourager les autres.* The Chief confided to my boy's care two women, captives. All the prisoners were fastened together by a cord through the lobe of the ears, and the Lhoosai set out with their plunder on the return journey. Now, one of the captive women was young, and not accustomed to walking; so after the first day's march her feet swelled, and she was unable to go further. The Chief therefore ordered that she should be speared. "Well," said the narrator, "I took the spear and went towards her, and Rutton Poia said, 'Do it neatly, I will look on,' for it was the first time I had ever speared any one. When the girl saw me take the spear and come towards her, she fell a-weeping, and caught my garments and my hands, and all my heart thumped, and I could not hurt her. It was pitiful! So the Chief began to laugh at me, and said, 'O white-livered, and son of a female dog, when we return to the village, I will tell the young maidens of your courage;' so I shut my eyes and speared her. My stroke was ill-directed, and she did not die; so the Chief finished the work, and he made me lick the spear. The blood of Bengallees is very salt. Since then I have not been afraid to spear any one."

Among the Lhoosai it is customary for a young warrior to eat a piece of the liver of the first man he kills; this, it is said, strengthens the heart and gives courage. The use of stimulants, as churrus, bhang, &c., to spur a man up for fight, is unknown among these tribes. In each tribe will be found some pre-eminently brave men; they are described as "not knowing pain or death." The weapons of the Lhoosai are the dâo, spear, and gun. I have seen no other among them. Gunpowder they obtain, it is said, from Burmah, and, until lately, from the Bengallees of Cachar and Chittagong. Latterly, however, increased vigilance on the part of the authorities has driven them to manufacture a rough sort of powder; they learnt to do this from the Shendoo tribe.

The custom of putting the village in quarantine is strictly observed by all the Lhoosai in case of sickness; and once a year, at the sprouting of the young rice, as a matter of religion. At the gathering of the harvest, they have a festival called among them "Chukchai." The Chief goes solemnly with his people into the forest, and cuts down a large tree, which is afterwards carried into the village, and set up in the midst. Sacrifice is then offered, and "khong," spirits, and rice, are poured over the tree. A feast and dance close the ceremony. The unmarried men and girls only are the dancers.

The Lhoosai cultivate by jooming in the

manner common to all hill tribes. They sometimes suffer severely from the inroads of rats, which again disappear as mysteriously and suddenly as they arrived. In carrying loads or cutting joom, the Lhoosai clear the lungs with a continuous "hau! hau!" uttered in measured time by all. Without making this sound, they say they would be unable to work. The village lads whistle with their fingers in a manner exactly similar to a London street boy. As a rule, they bathe but seldom, as their villages are generally situated at a long distance from water, and at an elevation which much reduces the temperature. They work in iron. A rough species of forge is found in every village, and they have made some progress in iron-working, having been taught by Bengallee captives to repair the lock of a gun, as also to make spear-heads and fish-hooks. They cannot, however, make a gun-barrel. They are ignorant of the art of making pottery. Their plates and bottles are the leaves of the jungle and gourds; they use brass and earthen vessels when they can obtain them either in war or by barter at the frontier bazaars. They smoke pipes of bamboo lined with copper or iron. They have no money current among them; but they are aware of its use, and employ it in purchasing articles in the frontier markets. They suffer sometimes from remittent fever. Boils are common among them, and sometimes inflammation of the bowels from over-drinking and eating; but, save these ailments, they were formerly unacquainted with disease. In 1861, however, they made a raid into British territory, and took back cholera with them. This disease excited the greatest terror, so much so, that numbers of the tribe put an end to their existence by suicide, blowing out their brains with their own guns on the first symptoms declaring themselves. They called it "the foreign sickness." In like manner they took back the small-pox among them from Kassalong Bazaar in 1860. They are ignorant of medicine; but if a man be very ill they offer sacrifice, and the "koa-vang" is consulted. I have never met or heard of an instance of goitre among the hill men, although I am told that persons in some of the Bengallee villages at the foot of the hills suffer from it. Syphilis is unknown. Diseases are sometimes attributed to witchcraft; and if the tribe declares this proven, the wizard is cut down without more ado.

On the death of a father of a family, notice is sent to all his friends and relatives. The corpse is then dressed in its finest clothes, and seated in the centre of the house in a sitting posture. At the right hand is laid the dead man's gun and weapons; on the left sits the wife weeping. All the friends assemble, and there is a big feast. Food is placed before the dead man, who sits upright and silent among them; and they address him, saying, "You are going on a long journey, eat." They also fill his pipe with tobacco, and place it between his lips. These ceremonies occupy twenty-four hours, and on the second day after death they bury the corpse. Among the Dhun and Khoon clans the body is placed in a coffin made of a hollow tree-trunk, with holes in the bottom. This is placed on a lofty platform, and left to dry in the sun. The dried body is afterwards rammed into an earthen vase and buried; the head is cut off and preserved. Another clan sheathe their dead in pith (solăh); the corpse is then placed on a platform, under which a slow fire is kept up until the body is dried. The corpse is then kept for six months to allow relatives and friends of every degree to come from a distance and take farewell of the deceased; it is then buried. The Howlong clan hang the body up to the house-beams for seven days, during which time the dead man's wife has to sit underneath spinning. She may not stir; and if friends do not bring her food, she must perforce starve.

It is curious to compare with the foregoing account a relation of the customs and manners of the Lhoosai Kookies given by a traveller in the last century. I transcribe it verbatim:—

[*From the French of M. Boucheseiche, who translated the original from the English of J. Rennel, Chief Engineer of Bengal. Upon the religion, the manners, laws, and the customs of the Cucis, or the inhabitants of the Tipra Mountains. Published at Leipsic in* 1800.]

"The nation which inhabit the hills to the east of Bengal give to the Creator of the world the name of Patyen, or Putchien. They believe that in every tree resides a deity, that the sun and moon are gods, and that the worship rendered by them to those deities of secondary importance is agreeable to Patyen, the Great Creator.

"If a man of this nation should happen to slay another, neither the Chief nor any of the relations of the deceased have the right of vengeance; but if his brother or other near relation chooses to kill the murderer, none have the right to prevent them. When a Cuci is taken in theft or any other crime, the Chief can compel him to reimburse the persons who have been injured by his misdeed; and, after giving his decision, the Chief is entitled to a fee. The criminal and the aggrieved parties are compelled to give a feast to their respective tribes. The Cucis formerly were not in the habit of killing all women found by them in the dwellings of their adversaries. The origin of the present barbarous custom is, indeed, singular enough. A woman, who was engaged working in the fields, asked another why she had come so late to her sowing. She replied, that her husband having just started on the war-path, she had been detained in preparing his food and other necessary arrangements. One of the enemies of the tribe heard her say this, and became very angry at learning that she had thus succoured one who had gone out to do injury to his people. He bethought himself, also, that if the women did not take care of the house and prepare their husbands' food when going on the war-path, there would be considerable inconvenience accruing. Since then, the Cucis always cut off the heads of the women of vanquished enemies; more especially are they murderously disposed to any who may be with child. A Cuci, who, in surprising a village, can kill a woman big with child, and obtain both her head and that of the unborn infant, is thought to have committed a most meritorious act, as with one blow he has destroyed two enemies.

"The marriage customs among this people are as follow:—When a rich man desires to take to wife a certain girl, he makes a present of four or five head of cattle (guyal) to her parents, and forthwith takes her to his house. Her parents kill the guyal, and having cooked much rice and brewed much liquor, they give a great feast to all their relations and kin. Poorer people follow the same custom in accordance with their means. Cucis are allowed to marry without regard to blood relationship: only a mother may not wed with her son. If a woman has a son by her husband, the marriage is indissoluble; but if they do not agree, and have no son, the husband can cast off his wife and take another. The Cucis have no idea of hell or heaven, or of any punishment for evil deeds, or rewards for good actions. They believe only that when a person dies, a being or spirit seizes his soul and carries it off. At the moment of its being carried off, whatever is named, the dead man will obtain and enjoy hereafter.

"This people eat the flesh of elephants, pigs, and other animals; and, if they happen to find a dead beast, they do not hesitate to dry its flesh for consumption. When a tribe determines to make war, they send out spies to discover the position and force of their enemy, as well as to find out the path. They then lay an ambush at night, and at two or three in the morning they fall upon the village to be cut up. Their weapons are the sword and lance, the bow and arrow. If an enemy abandons his village, they slay all the women and children who may fall into their hands, and carry off all they can lay hands on; but if the enemy, having learnt their design, has the courage to await and meet the onslaught, they quietly and quickly return to their homes.

"If the Cucis see a star very near the moon, they look upon it as a certain sign of an intended assault on their village, and they pass the night under arms. Often they lie in wait in the jungles and paths near their village, and kill any one who may present themselves.

"When the Cucis are thus ambushed, leech-bites or snake-bites will not draw the faintest cry from them nor make them quit their hiding-place; and the man who brings back the head of a foe is sure of universal applause.

"If two tribes, fighting hand to hand, see the victory uncertain between them, they make a signal to suspend the combat, send out ambassadors, and conclude a peace with a grand feast, taking sun and moon to witness the sincerity of their peace-making. But if one tribe is weaker than the other, and succumb in conflict, they are compelled to pay a yearly tribute in rice, cattle, slaves, or arms.

"In the field, the Cucis' provisions consist of yams and rice boiled to a cake in bamboos. They are thus enabled to dispense with cooking, and can make long and rapid marches; and they can perform in one day as much as an ordinary man can do in three or four. Arrived at the place which they wish to attack, they surround it during the night; and if they surprise it, they massacre, without pity, men, women, and children, reserving only such as they wish for slaves. They carry away the heads of the slain in leather sacks, and are careful, if possible, to keep their hands unwashed and bloody. The slaughter is always crowned by a big feast, where they indulge in the grim pleasantry of filling the dead mouths of the heads they have cut off with food, saying, 'Eat, appease your hunger and thirst. In the same way that I have slain you, may my children kill yours.' This feast is repeated a second time in the course of the expedition, and as often as possible news is sent to their village as to their success and the number of heads they have taken. Whenever it is known that heads have been obtained, the whole village evinces the liveliest satisfaction. They make head-dresses of red and black threads, embroidered with beads and all precious things; and taking with them large vessels of spirits, they go to meet the conquerors. During the journey they blow reedpipes, strike gongs, and make the woods resound with rude music. When they meet the conquerors, they break into song and dance, and give themselves up to the expression of the most frantic enjoyment. When a married man brings his wife a head, they pledge one another alternately in horns of liquor, and she even washes his bloody hands in the liquor that they drink.

"As soon as the conquerors reach their village, they assemble before the Chief's house, and make a pyramid of the heads they have taken. Round this monument of their victory they dance and drink until they generally fall from intoxication. They kill by the thrust of a spear some pigs and guyals, and make a fresh feast, in which the liquor is not spared. The principal men of the tribe place their enemies' heads on bamboo poles, which they place on the tombs of their ancestors. The man who brings most heads receives from the richest persons in the tribe presents of cattle and liquor; and when any of the enemy have been brought in alive, the chiefs who have not taken part in the expedition are allowed to slaughter these unhappy captives. Certain tribes in particular are the artificers of all warlike weapons, while others are quite ignorant of all handicraft.

"The women do all the house work. The men are employed in hunting, in cultivating, and in war. They know no division of time save from day to day. Five days after the birth of a male, and three days after that of a daughter, they give a feast to all their kin. The ceremony commences by the placing of a pole before the house; they then kill a guyal or pig, and drink is served out *ad libitum.* The day concludes with songs and dances. Those Cucis whom nature or accident renders incapable of reproduction keep no house; they live from door to door like religious mendicants. When one presents himself at the house of a rich man, the owner ties a long string of red and white stones to a bamboo. He gives alms to the mendicant, and feasts the village. They pay superstitious homage to those red and white stones.

"When a man dies, his relatives kill a pig or a guyal, and boil the flesh. They cover the corpse with a piece of cloth, pour a little liquor into its mouth, of which they all first partake, as a species of offering to the deceased's manes. This ceremony is repeated at intervals for many days. They afterwards place the body on a low platform of split bamboo. They pierce the corpse in several places, and light a slow fire underneath, so as to dry the body. They then wrap it in a shroud and bury it, and for a year afterwards they offer the first fruits of their crops on the tomb. Some tribes pay different honours to the dead. They cover the body in cloth and matting, and suspend it from the branches of a lofty tree. When the flesh is quite decomposed, they collect the bones, clean and preserve them in a vase, which they open on all important occasions, pretending that in thus consulting the bones, they are following the wishes of their deceased relative.

"A widow of this tribe is compelled to remain for a year beside the tomb of her deceased husband, her family bringing her food. If she dies during this year, they pay her funeral honours; if she survives, they re-conduct her to her house, and celebrate her return by a festival.

"When, in dying, a Cuci leaves three sons, the eldest and the youngest share the inheritance; the second has nothing. If he leaves no sons, his goods fall to his brothers; and if he has no brothers, they revert to the

Chief of the tribe. In the spring of 1776 many Cucis visited Mr. Charles Croftes, who was the Commandant for the English East India Company at Jafferabad. They appeared very satisfied with their reception, executed their dances, and promised to return after the harvest."

The Shendoo people is the last I shall have to mention. They indeed seem to be more a nation than a tribe; but the accounts and information of their habitudes possessed by us are scanty and insufficient. The little that we do know I proceed to set forth:— They inhabit the country north-east and east of the Blue Mountain, which is a conspicuous mark in the range which bounds the Hill Tracts south and east. It is said that the Lhoosai have been driven northward and westward by the Shendoos; they again may have been driven northward on to the Lhoosai by the stir and movement of the tribes to their south. They bind their hair in a very high and lofty knot over the forehead, and both male and female are distinguished by a decorum in the matter of dress that, from our knowledge of the other tribes, would hardly be expected.

The Shendoo women wear a short chemise of white home-spun cotton covering the bosom, and a long petticoat of dark-blue cotton stuff, reaching below the knee. Over the shoulders and head, when out of doors, they wear the fine cotton robe or cloth, for the manufacture of which they are pre-eminently distinguished: the cloth is black, with brilliant red and yellow stripes. The women bind their hair in smooth bands on each side of the face, fastening it in a knot at the back of the head. The men wear a cloth round their waist and a mantle of cotton cloth over their shoulders. Both sexes in stature are above the ordinary height of the hill men, and of a fairer complexion. The faces of those I have seen do not bear any signs of the prevailing Mongolian type of physiognomy. I am told that they do not cultivate with the dâo in joom fashion, but are acquainted with the method of terrace cultivation common among the Himalayan tribes; they use a large heavy hoe in breaking up the land for seed. They do not reap the grain with a sickle, but pluck the ears by hand. Field labour, as a general rule, is performed by the men: only the wives of very poor men labour in the fields. The Shendoo houses are raised from the ground, and built entirely of planks and logs of wood. The bamboo is said not to grow in that part of the country.

Iron is found in the Shendoo country. They make salt from brine springs existing in the country. They manufacture their own gunpowder. Sulphur they obtain from Burmah, and an inferior sort of saltpetre is collected from heaps of earth which they strongly impregnate with urine. Their guns do not appear to be of European manufacture; the stocks are painted red, black, and yellow, and are highly varnished. Their powder flasks are made of guyal horns, polished and beautifully inlaid with silver and ivory. The men smoke a pipe made of a joint of a bamboo, copper-lined. The women use a tiny hookah, also of copper, with a clay bowl. The tobacco water which collects in the bottom of the women's hookahs is held in high estimation among them as a preservative of the teeth and gums. Every man carries a small gourd full of it, and it is an act of common courtesy among them to present it to an acquaintance or visitor, in order that he may take a sip; just as among us, it used formerly to be customary to offer a neighbour a pinch of snuff. Their tobacco is fermented, pressed, and cut up, presenting exactly the appearance of our Cavendish tobacco. The Chiefs wear a thick plume of the tail feathers of the "beemraj" in their turbans. A slave among them is valued at eight muskets or two guyals. They appear to be ignorant of money or its value. Both the Shendoos and Lhoosai are to a man unable to swim or manage a boat: this is owing to their dwelling in the higher ranges of hills at the head waters of the rivers, where the stream is swift, shallow, and broken by rapids. They are said to worship four spirits, or deities, viz. Surpar, Patyen, Khosing, and Wanchang. Surpar is the head of all. They believe that after death they will live again in another country where there is no trouble, the trees bearing food, clothes, and every thing necessary for life. In addition to the four deities above named, they sacrifice to the spirits of earth and water on the occasion of their beginning to cultivate. They seem to have no distinctive names for these minor spirits. Their sacrifice to the water kelpie is a fowl killed and thrown into the river. For the earth-god meat and rice is left exposed on the ground. They have no priests; each man performs his own sacrifice; but as among the Lhoosai and Pankhos, they have men among them supposed to be the special favourites and oracles of their gods, and at certain times and seasons these men become possessed or filled by the divinity. They are monogamons, as a rule by choice; but a Chief or any other powerful man may marry his stepmother after his father's death. Marriage, as with all the tribes, is merely a matter of mutual consent, and is celebrated by feasting and dancing.

The Shendoo country is said to be very extensive, some fifteen days' journey across.

They procure ponies, cattle, and silks from the Province of Yan on the east, while to the north they are said to have communication with the British authorities of Cachar. The Shendoos bury their dead in a grave lined with stone. A Chief or a woman of any position is buried in a sitting posture as among the Bunjogees. With the body are interred its weapons, ornaments, and insignia of rank.

The tribes wearing their hair in a high knot over the forehead, as Shendoos, Bunjogees, and Kumi, are called Poy. The Shendoo tribe is called Lakheyr Poy in the Lhoosai tongue.

During the cold season of 1865 I undertook a journey into the Shendoo country, with a view to, if possible, entering into friendly relations with them, or at any rate to ascertain something definite concerning them. My experiences will, I think, be best set before my readers in the form of a diary kept by me during the expedition, which is as follows:—

" *29th November*, 1865.—We are camped on the fork of brawling hill stream among heaps of water-worn boulders. I am sitting on my mat under a great tree, which spreads over the stream. Half the party have gone road-hunting, the remainder are smoking cheroots and making baskets, while a select few are damming up one of the small streams hard by with ulterior views as to fish. Close by me, just on the edge of the water, are a number of young shoots of the sunn grass, which were stuck there at early dawn by the exploring party. The reason for this ceremony is a belief in the existence of a powerful water Kelpie, who inhabits the streams of the Twine Kheong, and to whom they make peace offerings. Each man having his green shoot in hand, the Roaja[2] goes ankle deep into the water, the others standing on the marge, and offers up some sort of prayer or invocation for success. This done, each man plants his grass shoot, and they go away satisfied. I gave the son of the chief Roaja a lesson on

[2] Roaja—a village head-man or leader.

the fiddle last night, to the intense delight of all the others who sat round, and upon my word the lad made a very good beginning. If I were located here, I think a stringed band would not be an impossibility. These people have a capital ear for rhythm and time. I served out to them to-day half my store of salt pork, and at this moment great is the frizzling in pots and sniffing of noses that is going on. They eat also frogs, young plantain shoots, and the tops of fern leaves, such at least is part of to-day's bill of fare. We all dined off plantain leaves and drink out of bamboo cups; the table equipage had to be abandoned when we commenced marching. Twekam Tonlyn, head of Lama Kheong people, promises me a gecko steak on the first opportunity. I dare say it will be very good. I know they eat them in the West Indies.

"1st *December*, 1865.—I could not write yesterday, I was so tired. We started at early morning, and to the top of Ranrong Tong we followed the survey road, which was easy enough, although trying to the back sinews.

When, however, we got to the top we struck off to the north into a wild elephant track. This we followed for about two miles, and then we had to cut our way through bamboo jungle. We had two precipices to go down, in the doing of which it is a wonder no one was killed. The stones came rattling about one's ears like hail, and one had to hang on by roots and to grass in the most dangerous manner, with a fall of I don't know how many feet below. At 4 p.m., however, dead beat, we all reached a Kumi village on the Sungoo side. I got a touch of fever here, the result of my last ten days' diet of rice, water, and fish.

"There is a stone near the Sungoo not far off the embouchure of Teendoo Kheong, on which is an inscription in an unknown language, the people say it is a magical incantation that was set up by a Burmese Raja a hundred years ago.

"During my yesterday's march I noticed wild thyme, parsley, celery, and sage in the jungle; also for about a mile a tract of wild coffee. On the jooms here and there are melons, cucumbers, rice, genara, grain, &c. Soil seems first-rate, like garden mould. We also fell in with a troop of Huluq monkeys.

"It would be a good plan, I think, to distribute English seeds among these hill people. Our advanced posts should be furnished with a few rockets; the hill people fear them much. Prevalent diseases—rheumatism, eye diseases, fever, and diarrhœa. Some gaudy-coloured ear-rings are wanted for presents, in shape truncated cone-hollow. The language of the people of this part is beginning to change. They only understand Mughi slightly. The village here is situated in a bend of the Teendoo Kheong, and surrounded on all sides with high hills. The people wear slightly more clothing than those on the Mahamoree side, but the women still have but the one waistcloth and pewter girdle. They drink the universal seepah of fermented rice. A big jar of it was brought me this morning. They were greatly pleased at my drinking. You suck it up through a reed, like sherry cobbler. It is slightly acidulated in taste, and by no means unpleasant.

"Moved on down the Teendoo Kheong to the banks of the Sungoo. In the Kheong there was one rather striking place, which made me stop to look at it. It seemed as if half a large hill had topped bodily into the small stream, and that too quite recently, for the rent face of the rock was fresh and bare, without a sign of vegetation. I should have liked to see the fall; its magnitude I could appreciate by the immense fragments of *débris* over which we with difficulty made our way. Our camp at the Sungoo was lonely swift rapids, long stretches of calm water just simmering into streaks of silver, like a wind-flaw, on the brink of the falls and the banks, such moss-grown overhanging rocks, water-worn and fern-plumed—it was a feast of beauty. Towards evening my party brought four boats, hired at two annas a-day, and cheap too. As soon as they arrived, I proceeded to shoot the rapids; and anything more exciting cannot be conceived.

I thought we were in for a ducking race, but we scraped through amid shouts of laughter from my Mroongs, who stood on the bank smoking their pipes and watching 'the ashiang' handle a paddle. In the bed of the stream to-day my men amused themselves looking for fish when we halted. They peeped cautiously about, and then putting their hands under a rock, just as boys tickle trout at home in England, they would produce a great eel-like fish, white-bellied, and his back mottled with brown and black.

"*Memorandum.*—Presents prized by these people would be some wooden cheroot-holders and some wax matches in small tin boxes.

"*3rd December*, 1865.—Halted at Ramakree Kheong—a very heavy day's work. Passed no less than twelve rapids; the first two or three were exciting, but afterwards it became a bore. The importance of a thorough knowledge of Burmese cannot be over-estimated; it irks me like a seton in the neck to feel myself at the mercy of my interpreters. I know enough to give orders and make myself understood, but when it comes to a council, I hobble hopelessly in the rear. I wish to goodness I had brought no escort at all. Bengallees are worse than useless in the hills; they are vile, cumbersome lumber, which eats largely, and is not even pretty to look at. I would send them back even now, but there may be need for them, and it's a pity after having brought them so far, to send them back just as I get to the place where they may be needed. We passed the Fairy's Stone to-day ("Nye Kyak"), not the one with the inscription which I could not visit, but a great square mass of rock standing up alone in the middle of the river, its sides terraced as if by men's hands; but this, I suppose, is merely the action of the water on the cleavage of the strata. Further on was a castle-like crag on the left bank; this is called the Joomeah's Rock. They say that it is filled with rupees, which were buried there by a village of Joomeahs, who were carried off by the Shendoos, *en masse*, into slavery.

"*4th December*, 1865.—From Ramacree Kheong to Modhocree Kheong, a long day's journey. The camp not settled until nightfall, and without food all day. We live now in true jungle fashion; my plates are plantain leaves, my cooking-pots bamboo choongas. Dinner good nevertheless, consisting of fish freshly caught, two slices salt pork, oatmeal cake, a dish of fern-tops, and a curry of the young shoots of wild plantain.

"Tiger spoor all round the camp, as well as dung. Had a general inspection of arms, &c.; found all fit for service. We ascended some light rapids to-day. After passing Singopha the river gets less rocky and narrower. I stopped at Singopha to see the fort. It consists of some dozen of old posts lying rotting in a thick jungle. The post has not been occupied for two years. There are no houses from Ramacree upwards. The great difficulty in a journey like this is the conveyance of food. It takes more men to carry their own and my party's food than all the traps put together. A party of the hill people joined us to-day, and asked to travel with us to the Koladyne for protection.

"*5th December*, 1865.—From Modhocree, over Moddo Tong, down the Tumtoo Kheong, to the Pee Kheong River. There was a sort of path by which we came, but it has been a hard day's work; sometimes cutting a way, sometimes creeping on hands and knees, then wading knee-deep in water. Leeches there were in myriads. Although I had thick woollen socks, and shooting boots with trousers and gaiters over all, no less than eight managed to draw blood; and, as for the men, they were covered with them. As we were going along on one side of a ravine, on the other, through the bamboos, we saw a magnificent elephant going slowly up the opposite hill. I did not fire at him, as he could not be effectually hurt, and it would only have been giving pain needlessly. At the junction of the Tumtoo Kheong, with the Pee Kheong right in our path, we found two arrows set trap-fashion, with a spring. I was on ahead with my Mugh servant, so we quietly removed them, and said nothing to the others. I, however, loaded the whole party, and put on double sentries; it might have been accidental, but one cannot be too cautious. I was stung several times by nettles to-day, the first I have seen in the country. They are just like an English nettle seen through a magnifying-glass. The people on the Sungoo say that fever is most prevalent with them in October and November at the end of the rains. The Roajas were talking to me to-night. They say they will come and see me at Chittagong. I must try and get the Commissioner to let me have a small guest-house built, as when these people know me, I do not doubt they would frequently come in if they had anywhere to go to. I tried to get them to send me one or two of their sons to live with me, but as yet they are afraid. They have no written character. I should like to introduce the English letters among them, and it could be done without difficulty.

"The people say that from the source to

the junction of the Pee Kheong with the Koladyne there is not a single inhabitant. Two hundred years ago the valley was thickly populated, but the Kookies and Shendoos have emptied it.

"*6th December*, 1865.—To-day we left the Pee Kheong by Lama Kheong, wading up, crossed a spur of the Pee Kheong range, named Kanka Tong, then down again across a tributary of Pee Kheong, and so over the main range of Eynko Tong. Much the same journey as yesterday. We halted at Teyn Kreyng. Roaja Rhoma, caste Khoomee, course east, and then east by south. Teyn Kreyng is on the Khoo Kheong falling into the Koladyne. The village is not stockaded, but they had a most extraordinary stronghold in a tree. The hut was capable of holding some twenty people, and made shot-proof by strong billets of wood, looped all round and in the floor. I went up, but the passage seemed very perilous; my foot went through the bamboos twice, and the whole affair shook fearfully. The people here are much subject to boils; they treat them by the actual cautery. A bad-looking set they are, these men, and dishonest to boot. They said they knew nothing of the Shendoos; but they had some pretty little hookahs, which the women smoked, and I wanted to buy one, and they talking about it in their own tongue, which one of my men understood, although they did not know it. Heard that they had brought them from the Shendoo country, and could not replace them, so they concluded not to let me have a hookah. Their village, being all alone too, is suspicious. Depend upon it, they are in league with the Shendoos. Could get no assistance here.

"They say that there are villages three days' journey up the Pee Kheong to the north. There is a track that leads to them nearly opposite to Teendoo Kheong on the Sungoo. Here is another expedition in embryo. I am sick of my escort, and shall send them back to-morrow by Akyab. A Bengallee is no more use than a log of wood in these hills. They are nearly all footsore, ailing, and what is worse, grumbling. No European has been in these parts or up the Pee Kheong[3].

"*Akyab, 1st February*, 1866.—Having been so unfortunate during my recent expedition into the Hill Tracts of the Upper Koladyne as to lose the whole of my books, papers, memoranda, &c., I am compelled to supply their place, as far as lies in my power, by recording from memory the most salient events of the last six weeks. My last diary was sent back by me from the junction of the Khoo Kheong and Koladyne, a little below Tulukmee, whence I also dispensed with the services of the main body of my small escort which had so far accompanied me from

[3] The first part of my diary concluded here, and I sent it back to the Commissioner of Chittagong by the hands of my useless Bengallee escort of constables. We had arrived at the river Koladyne, and I saw no further use for them, but rather hindrance. I also dismissed here all my Mahamoree Roajas and coolies; they, honest fellows, being content to take my I. O. U. instead of pay. I had left with me one head constable, a cook, and two Mugh interpreters.—T. H. L.

Chittagong. My object in doing this was two-fold:—*First*, to lessen the very heavy expense which the carriage of our food alone gave rise to; and *secondly*, because I was of opinion that my being attended by even a small number of armed men might give rise to suspicion on the part of the hill tribes and perhaps hinder my movements. It was, I think, the 8th of December when I arrived at Tulukmee. I had with me one head constable, Phusla, a Punjabee, and the two interpreters, Cox Bazaar men, who had come with me from Chittagong. The inhabitants of the place received us with caution. They feared two things: 1*st*, the consequences, from the Shendoos; 2*nd*, that the Akyab authorities might take umbrage. I explained that I had no intention of interfering with the Akyab authorities, and indeed had come over by invitation to attend a conference of hill tribes that was to be held here, I understood, in January. They said that they knew nothing of any conference, and saw but little of any sahibs up in these parts. They seemed very averse to helping me at all. However, I went into the village, ate and drank with them, distributing a few small presents, and the talk lasted far into the night. The 'Katungree,' or head man of the village, was old, sick, and a nonentity; although his sons, two likely lads, will be good for something eventually. One of these boys had been a prisoner for two years among the Shendoos, whence he had been ransomed by a payment of eight muskets. I offered him a head constableship; he would be useful in our Hill Tracts. The man who seemed to have the most influence in the village was one Khiloo, a Doctor, supposed to be possessed of magic powers and great wisdom. His father had formerly been the Government 'Kyun,' or revenue collector on the Koladyne, and with him my arrangements were carried on. They fleeced me heavily by-the-bye here on account of provisions, every thing seeming to be at famine price. They said they had not suffered from a Shendoo raid for some years; that formerly the village was small and had few inhabitants, but that now there were many men, although they admitted that in case of an attack the entire population would take to their boats, where, they said, the Shendoos could not follow them. It was a curious fact, and one that was borne out by my after-experience, that the Shendoos appear to be unable to manage a boat, or even to swim. All their journeyings and fightings are exclusively by land. Tulukmee is on the left bank of the river going up; it numbers, I should say, some 300 inhabitants, and there are about fifty houses. The people are Kheongthas, or sons of the river; in other words, inland Mughs. They speak the Rakhaing dialect, but all of them are also well acquainted with the Koomee *patois*. A Koonaee village is close by, almost in fact one with the Kheongtha settlement. The Koomees are incurably nomadic, but these Kheongtha villages seem to remain very long in the same place. This I attribute to the fact of their carrying on some small system of barter or trade in cotton and cloth in addition to the subsistence they derive merely from agriculture. I noticed that several of the finer descriptions of foreign cotton had been introduced by the Akyab authorities; the plants, however, did not seem to have much favour in the eyes of the inhabitants, being merely cultivated, exceptionally, near the houses. They said the foreign plant was not hardy enough and required too much attention, indeed the indigenous staple appeared to me to be very fine, almost matchless in colour and apparently of long fibre. A system of hybridization, if possible, I should think, would prove serviceable. It was agreed at length that Khiloo would accompany me up the river to see the country and gain what information I could. In the morning, however, there was such delay in starting that it was not until with our own hands we had shouldered and carried down our baggage that we managed to get off. Khiloo appeared in full fig. Round his head a thin muslin turban twisted rope fashion and showing the grizzled topknot of hair which he wore in common with all Mughs. His chupkun, or robe of black satin, somewhat tarnished, but still very presentable, a dhotee or potoho of dark purple and black silk, while a Burmese cutlass in a wooden sheath was tucked under his arm. He wore suspended round his neck the silver pincers and appendages for trimming the beard which all these people use.

"We were to go first to the village of one Yuong, who was a Koomee Chief or Toungmeng of some influence, a short day's journey up the river; thither accordingly, through the dense morning fog, we bent our way. The fog in these parts commences on the river at about 2 a. m., and does not lift until mid-day; the cold, too, now began to be something intense. Our boats were the usual wooden dug-outs propelled by paddles in the deeps and poled along by men in the bow through the shallows and up the rapids, which now became somewhat numerous and dangerous. Arrived at Yuong's we found that he was not in the village, or at least the people said so. I, however, got out of the boats and installed myself in his house, stating my intention to remain there until he honoured me with an interview. This man's house was altogether unique in its way, and by far the finest and best-built dwelling I had ever seen in the Hill Tracts. It was built in the usual fashion about five feet from the ground with a platform in front, where the bamboo water tubes, &c., were placed, the platters cleaned, &c. The house itself consisted of one immense hall or atrium and an enclosed platform at the back. This hall was at least 50 feet long by 20 broad, with two large fireplaces made in the usual way of loose earth battened into a square at either end; the walls were double with an interval of about 18 inches between. Outside and along the whole plinth above the door ran a line of skulls of deer, the guyal and the bear, all smoked to one uniform dark brown tinge, for this was the custom of the people, and I was told that Yuong was a mighty hunter. Inside the house in the centre towered up another trophy of horns and skins, including buffalo horns of large size, and mixed with weapons, shields, powder-horns, and spears. I regret much that I lost my diary, for I obtained here much information as to the people, their diseases, average length of life, religious ceremonies and belief, together with the names of their months, system of days, numerals, about 300 words of the language; all, however, is gone, and my memory fails me. This man, Yuong, is at feud with the Shendoos. The occasion of his quarrel I ascertained here, and afterwards verified in the Akyab Police Office. It appears that some time ago a Shendoo chief sent an embassy to Kounglaphroo, or, as we call him, 'the Poang,' consisting of six men, bearing ivory and home-spun cloths. Of these men five were murdered by Kounglaphroo's orders, and the man who escaped was captured and slain by Yuong on his way back to his tribe. For this reason it was that the Shendoos made raids on the Chittagong frontier, and are at enmity with Yuong. He has burnt one of their villages, and they have returned the compliment twice over to him. Yuong himself soon came in, and from him I gained most of my information. He is a young man, not more than thirty I should say, with a somewhat crafty expression of face. I should not like to trust him.

"He had living with him two slaves, one Langtoo Mooroong, known at Karyoung Roa, on the Proda Kheong (*vide* Report of Superintendent, 'Hill Tracts,' on raid made in December, 1864), who he had either taken or brought from the Shendoos, whose language he spoke, besides Koomee and Rakhaing. The dialect of Arracan, both here and in our own district, is the universal '*lingua franca*,' spoken and understood by every one. One of these slaves was a Mroo, from Chittagong side; he could speak little Bengallee, but was careful to hide his accomplishment, which only oozed out when he was under the influence of liquor.

"From Young Roa we went on to Teynwey

Roa, the residence of Teynwey, the furthermost tribute-paying chief on the Akyab frontier. Here I halted. The village itself consists of some fifty houses, and is situated on the top of a hill about 500 feet high. It was the first place I had yet seen that was regularly fortified. The approach to it was only by one side, and here you were met by a triple gateway; the doors were of solid three-inch timber, while a treble stockade of bamboo, covered from top to bottom with a perfect labyrinth of spikes, offered a somewhat formidable obstacle to any attacking party. Like all these hill villages, however, the position would be quite untenable before any competent assailants; a rocket or two, or even a fire-tipped arrow, would burn the village to the ground. There were lofty look-out stations placed all round the *enceinte* of the village, and the steep slopes adjacent were also defended by sharp *chevaux de frise* of pointed bamboo, as well as by 'poees' strewn in the ravines. The old chief Teynwey soon made his appearance, with a somewhat numerous following. He was unarmed, save for an enormous pipe which he carried in his hand. He wore a fine Shendoo cloth and turban, and in the latter was fixed a thick plume, consisting of the slender tail-feathers of the 'bhimraj.' The inhabitants of his village are one-half Koomees, the remainder are Kyaws. This latter tribe, or rather family, is curious, inasmuch as this is the only place where they are known to exist. Their physiognomy and dress also are unlike those of the Koomees. They have also a separate chief of their own. The most noticeable difference in their appearance was that the men, instead of wearing their hair like the Koomees or Mroos in a knot on the forehead, invariably tie it up behind in a club like the Cingalese. The women also wear their hair in a plaited coronet over the forehead. As I was talking to Teynwey another Chief made his appearance. He was the head of a small community of Shendoos (the only one in our limits), who resided close by and paid tribute to Government. He brought eggs and fowls as a present, and was accompanied curiously enough by four women of his tribe. I gave him some small presents, and learnt all I could from him. He could speak no language save his own. He was a powerful, rough-looking old fellow, with a thick stubble of a beard all over his chin (he shaved with a dâo, by-the-bye, so he said). His dress was not in any very marked degree different from that of other hill men, save that the turban was wound in a very high sort of tower or excrescence over the forehead. This head-dress, by the way, was distinctive of all the Shendoos I saw afterwards.. The women, on the contrary, were in every way different from those of the other tribes. In the first place they seemed to have some regard for decency, as they wore a kind of short habit shirt or shift and a petticoat of similar material. They also wore over the shoulders the usual fine striped Shendoo cloth, which is very handsome, although home-spun. Their hair was brought carefully in bands on each side of the face, fastening in a knot behind at the back of the head. The physiognomy of the whole party was different from that of the Koomees, the women, indeed, reminding me of nothing more than a Portuguese half-caste. The eyes, in particular, were well-shaped, with nothing of the Mongol type about them.

"On my presenting a present of some beads and a looking-glass to the oldest and chief dame of the party, she acknowledged my courtesy with a gracious smile, and in return drawing a small bottle-shaped gourd from some recess in her garments, she presented it to me to drink. On inquiry this appeared to contain the lees or dirty water from the bottom of the small Shendoo hookah which all the women smoke, and this poisonous decoction is held in high esteem by the men as a preservative for the teeth and gums. I was told not to swallow the nauseous abomination, but merely to rinse my mouth with it. On giving the old fellow some liquor to drink, I was surprised to notice that he would not touch it until the women had first partaken thereof, and in faith they required severally a great deal of pressing before they would drink. The old man told me that many of the Shendoos would like to come and settle in British limits, but that the revenue demanded from them was the great hindrance. In their own country, he said, five days' journey from here, they paid no tribute to their Chiefs, but lived together in community, the only acknowledgment of fealty being that each male was bound to give to the Chief a third of all flesh killed by him either in hunting or for home consumption, and also to follow him upon any warlike expedition; in return for this the Chief was bound to provide his followers with salt. He also confirmed the story I had previously heard as to the reason of the Shendoos' hostility to the Poang, but he said there were many Chiefs in his nation, some were friends of Kounglaphroo and some enemies. The Loungtsweys were a powerful tribe to the north-east of Chittagong, who were on friendly terms with the Poang.

"On his taking his departure with the women folk he requested me as a favour to fire my gun over their heads as they went, and with this wish I complied much to their satisfaction. At night I went up into the village to sleep, more especially as there was to be a grand dance, feast, and consultation as to me and my purposes. I was lodged in old Teynwey's house, and after dinner, which by-the-bye comprised, among other things, snake, flesh, and elephant's feet, the kyaw dance commenced. The music consisted of a rough kind of guitar, thrummed across by a bamboo stick, in shape not unlike a large fiddle, but made of one solid lump of wood, with wooden feet tied down the stem like a guitar. Drums of course *ad libitum.* The dance was simple enough, being performed by about twenty young fellows marching round in a circle to measured time. The rhythm, indeed, of the measure was wonderfully well marked, and just about the same as a stage triumphal march. The leader of the circle held in his hand a pretty little 'dâo' with a brazen handle bedizened with a long flowing tuft of scarlet goat's hair, the other performers bore some a shield, some an ordinary dâo, and these weapons were clanked together as the dancers moved. One step a pause, two steps all sink down on their hams and rise again, another step, then a jump, and a shout, and so on; I meanwhile putting in an 'obligato' accompaniment with fiddle and voice.

"In an adjoining room were the drinkers. Here two rows of pots were filled with the 'khoung' or 'seepah,' of which they are so fond, and to every pot were two or three men waiting for their turn at the reed through which the liquor is sucked. It is by no means an unpleasant drink; indeed, I got to like it very much before I left the hills, but, like all brews, there are sorts.

"Next day I abandoned the village, being driven out by the legions of bugs and other vermin with which the place was swarming, and proceeded to take up my abode in a little shanty or hut which they constructed for me below on the banks of the river. Meantime the conference had been held, and it was decided after sundry experiments in divination by Khiloo, that I was to be assisted. Accordingly it was determined that after due sacrifice to the Water Kelpie a deputation of six men should go to Kheynung's village (the largest in the Shendoo country), and endeavour to prevail upon him to come down and escort me to his residence. The sacrifice was performed in this wise; a goat was tied by the neck and another cord was attached to his hind legs; these cords being kept tight, she was thrown into an extended position. Then I took one cord, while the other was held by the five Chiefs; Yuong bearing the brazen-hilted dâo stood in the midst over the goat, and taking in his hand a small cup of liquor he took a mouthful and blew it out over me, then another mouthful over the Chiefs, and a third over the sacrifice, at the same time raising his dâo in the air and in a loud voice addressing an invocation to the river spirit; a few hairs were plucked from the goat and cast to the wind, and then with one stroke of the dâo he severed the goat's head from the body. The warm blood on the weapon was then smeared by him on my forehead and naked feet, and on those of all who had taken part in the ceremony. I was now informed that any one of us who acted falsely would be slain at once by his colleagues without more ado. This at any rate was decisive, and so after a big feed on the flesh of the goat, together with another which was slaughtered, and for both of which I had to pay, the messengers bearing with them presents from me departed for the Shendoo country, leaving me to await for the next twelve days the result of their mission. This preliminary of obtaining permission was made a *sine quâ non* by Teynwey and all the other Chiefs. Without it they said our lives would not be worth a moment's purchase in the Shendoo country, and although I pressed hard to get on I could not get a single man to go with me.

"The next day I was sitting in my little shanty playing my fiddle, when one of the guides I had brought with me discharged my gun close outside and sent the ball into me, wounding me in the thigh. It entered a little below the hip and came out just above the knee, and as the wound looked serious and gave me great pain, I felt myself obliged to go down to Akyab and obtain the services of the Doctor. It was not so much the pain I suffered, or the danger I was in, that made me thoroughly wretched, but that after going through so much privation my labour would now be fruitless, or that at any rate some one else would get the credit of it.

"I was wounded on the 15th of December at evening, and arrived in Akyab on the 20th at mid-day, having met Captain Munro, the Superintendent of Police, on my way down. He was out on tour and returned with me to his head-quarters. Here we found Colonel Phayre, the Chief Commissioner of British Burmah. I was of course unable to call upon him, but I wrote reporting all I had done and also forwarded my diary for his perusal. He was good enough to express satisfaction at my report, and to say that it would be proper for me to accompany Captain Munro up the Koladyne on my recovery, supposing that the Chittagong authorities approved of my so doing. I accordingly telegraphed to the Commissioner of Chittagong, and received his assent to the proposed arrangement.

"On the 5th of January, although my wound was still open, I was sufficiently recovered to make a fresh start.

"Colonel Phayre himself accompanied us some 250 miles, and held two conferences with the Hill chiefs on the way. He determined that a Superintendent of Akyab Hill Tracts should be appointed, and also that the tax paid by our tribute-paying tribes should be decreased. The following assessment will prevail for the future:—

"For every married man and family, two rupees a year.

"For every dâo used in clearing, one rupee yearly. Cripples, men over sixty years of age, are altogether exempt. Unmarried men to pay the dâo tax only. Any tribes from beyond our frontier coming to settle would not be required to pay tribute for two years. These rates apply to the Keongthas only. The other hill tribes, as Koomees and Mroos, at the rate of one rupee per annum for each house or family.

"These arrangements will, to a certainty, draw a great number of our people from Chittagong to the Koladyne.

"The custom of Goung-hpo, or price of a head, as it exists among all the hill tribes, is curious, and more especially noteworthy, as it is either the cause or pretext of every raid that is committed. The custom may be briefly described as the enforcement of demands, either of claims made by one tribe on another, for 'ata' or revenue, or for the price of the body of some deceased member of the community called Goung-hpo. The latter is the most frequent pretext, it being the practice among them, on the death of any inhabitant of their village, to saddle his death upon some other tribe or clan whose village the deceased may recently have visited, and then to demand a certain price for his life. This custom is but too often a cloak for mere robbery of the most violent description, in which both men and women are carried off as slaves.

"It is, however, a practice among them, in borrowing money, to give some relative as bodily security for repayment; care should, therefore, be taken in listening to any complaints as to slavery, that the voluntary bondage of the security is not misrepresented to be the forcible detention of a captive. The tribute of the hill tribes in Arracan is not paid exclusively in cash, but often in the shape of ivory and other country produce. Colonel Phayre, Captain Munro, and myself reached Tulukmee on the 12th January, whence, after staying one day, the Chief Commissioner left us with instructions to go as far as we could into the Shendoo country, and to endeavour to make friends with the chiefs of the principal tribes, as also, if possible, to prevail upon them to discontinue for the future all raids upon the Akyab and Chittagong frontiers. We were to obtain what information we could as to the British subjects in captivity; but on this point no direct steps as to ransom or release were to be taken, pending the result of our trip and further orders. We halted at Tulukmee for five days, sending on messengers and presents to the Shendoos' country to obtain permission to advance. We should have been detained longer than this, but fortunately news of my first visit and the motives thereof had reached the village of Khenung, a considerable Chief among them, and he had sent his second son, with five others of the tribe, down to Teynwey's village to reconnoitre. Our messengers, therefore, going up met this small party of Shendoos coming down, and with a great deal of difficulty prevailed upon them to come down the river as far as Tulukmee to meet us. They were very suspicious and frightened, but eventually made their appearance with old Teynwey. The interview was satisfactory. The Chief's son, Aylong, said there was no objection to our going into their country, but that we must pay for it to the tune of sundry brazen vessels, red cloths, beads, &c. These stipulations, after some haggling, we at length agreed to, and then Munro was informed that it was indispensable that all parties concerned should take an oath of friendship and alliance. Accordingly a fine fat young heifer was procured and slaughtered, in the same manner and with the same ceremonies as I have before described, with this exception, that the offering was tied to a thick stake set fast in the ground, and thrust through with a spear.

"On the 18th, then, we started once more on our upward course. The Shendoos would not go in a boat, but made their way by preference through the jungle on the river's bank, or when we came to any deep and impassable part of the river they would jump into my boat for five minutes, leaving it again as soon as possible. I was great friends with them by this time, and noted down a large number of their words and phrases. They were never tired of examining me and my belongings; the fiddle, lucifer matches, my writing materials and books apparently afforded them endless topics of conversation, but what most of all seemed to astonish them was my white skin. Aylong would take my hand and examine it attentively, then he would put it down carefully and stroking me on the shoulder say 'apa, aputlah,' it is good, it is fair. They gave me of their tobacco too, and this was a most welcome gift, as my stock had long ago run out. The tobacco they smoke is fermented, pressed and cut up just like our American Cavendish, and is by no means bad smoking. We halted nowhere now but pushed steadily on, passing Teynwey's on the 19th. Beyond his village we found three settlements of Khoons. These tribes are independent. In outward appearance, however, both they and their women very much resemble the Koomees of the Upper Koladyne. I noticed among them two men, who curiously enough had long brown beards, although in all other respects thorough hill men and claiming pure descent. I imagine, however, they must have had a cross of Bengallee blood in them, probably from captives taken in some raid. The women here wore large circular horn earrings, distending the lobe of the ear to an enormous size in true Koomee fashion. After passing the Khoom villages, which were all on hills, and with some attempt at fortification, we proceeded some two hours up the river until we arrived at the entrance of the Sullah Kheong, on the east bank of the Koladyne. The direction of the stream was about N. N. E., and we found considerable difficulty in getting our boats up it at all, as the water in some places was very shallow, and in one instance we had to land all our traps and draw the canoes up a small fall of about 4 feet. That same evening we arrived at Tawoo Kheong, a small streamlet running into the Sulla Kheong. Here our Shendoo guides informed us that we must leave our boats and strike inland. The coolies built themselves huts of plantain leaves on the bank, but Munro and self slept in our canoes. Next morning there was of course a great delay in starting. Munro finding that he had brought too many things, and that there were not sufficient coolies, therefore all superfluities were discarded, such as cooking pots, some provisions, with the heavier part of the presents, and concealed in the jungle, the Shendoos saying they would send people to fetch them when we reached their village. Our road lay in a N. E. direction, and was through the densest jungle. The guides showed wonderful sagacity in finding, or rather following, the path. Indeed there was no path, although they seemed to see one. True, for perhaps a mile here and there we would follow an elephant track, but the whole jungle was cut up with elephant roads, and there was no telling one from the other.

"Towards evening we halted on the banks of the Sulla Kheong. We appeared to have crossed a loop of country; indeed they told us that the stream made a long circuit to the east.

"The men ran up a small hut for Munro and self, and here we slept on the ground Next day we started early in a due north direction, and after travelling about six hours over very much the same kind of ground as the day before, we suddenly met three Shendoos, two of whom were armed with muskets, while one carried a spear. The Shendoos who were with us entered into conversation with them, and after a little while we learnt that they were the scouts of a large party which was some distance off. The three men seemed uneasy and disinclined to talk, being evidently suspicious of treachery. They were well armed with English Tower-marked flint muskets of King George's time. From the appearance of the stocks, however, I should imagine that the barrels had been re-stocked by themselves. Their powder horns were made of guyal's horns, beautifully inlaid and ornamented with silver and ivory. We now, through our interpreter, informed the strangers who we were and where we were going, viz., to the village of Kyannan or Kheynung, bearing presents and with peaceful intent, and we requested permission to proceed. They replied that they must get their Chief's orders first, and on this one of our Shendoo guides went with them to obtain permission. Two of the strangers returned shortly after and persuaded Aylong to go with them also. They were followed at a short interval by our other two Shendoos, so we were now left alone with only the hill men, coolies, &c., and they began to chatter vehemently together, putting down their loads and evidently in a fright about something. Yetshee, one of our friendly Shendoos, now returned and told us that there was a body of 3 to 400 Shendoos in front, and that they were on the war-path, so we had better be prepared.

"He said they were men from the following villages:—Moungtoo, Tunkran, Roupee Yonoo, all Shendoos, and that they were accompanied by some Lootsways from Chittagong. They were going to attack a village called Khoon. Thus much he said, and then went off into the jungle. Old Teynwey now seemed alarmed, and advised us to retire, but we did not think there was any danger and determined to wait awhile. Presently five of the stranger Shendoos were seen coming through the jungle. They said they were looking for Aylong, who had run into the jungle, and began to call him, but without effect. I then proposed that I should go forward with them and see the Chiefs, with a view to friendship; but this Munro would not hear of. In the meantime the Koomee coolies had, one by one, lifted their loads and taken the back track. Old Teynwey now entered into conversation with the Shendoos, and seemed to be entreating them. Several times he took the hand of the leader, and tried to place it on his forehead; but the Shendoo would not do what he required, and so Teynwey, without more ado, quietly took his departure also. We now began to think that there really was some danger. We were but six in all, viz., Lieutenant Munro, myself, my orderly, two constables, orderlies of Lieutenant Munro, and a Bengallee Khitmutgar, the latter being unarmed. On the other hand, one by one, the Shendoos had straggled up till they numbered about twenty men, and we could see more coming through the jungle. Four of the Shendoos were now seen to go behind a tree and commence priming their muskets, and another man deliberately levelled his piece at Lieutenant Munro and myself as we stood together. One of our constables, seeing this threatening gesture, immediately covered the Shendoo with his musket, and this made him lower his weapon. Almost immediately afterwards, two Shendoos rushed upon my orderly and attempted to wrest his carbine from him; and one of them tried to do the same with my gun, but they were repulsed, and were not successful in their endeavour. Seeing now that they had openly declared themselves hostile, we judged it expedient to retreat, and so went backwards with levelled guns, while the Shendoos rapidly took cover behind the trees and commenced priming. We were careful not to fire, as nearly all our ammunition was with the baggage. I had myself only four cartridges. We thus retreated, until the jungle becoming somewhat thicker, we turned and went at the double, in the hopes of overtaking some of our coolies and procuring a guide, for in the pathless wilderness in which we were, one could but have a very general idea of the road we had followed. We had not gone far, however, when we became aware that the enemy were out-flanking us, as men could be heard and seen on our right and left. A very little time after this we heard two shots, directly in our front, and concluded that the Shendoos had surrounded us. We halted for a few breathless moments, and held a hurried council, when all agreed it would be better to conceal ourselves in the jungle. For myself, I could not have gone much further at the rapid rate at which we had been travelling, with an open wound on my thigh, and having only recently been able to walk at all, it was hardly to be wondered at. Turning, then, from the path to the right, we crept into a small ravine in the heart of the jungle, densely overgrown with thorny bushes and long grass. Here we agreed to remain until night-fall, and then under cover of the darkness we hoped to escape. We had forgotten, however, that although the darkness could hide us, it would also hide from us all traces of the direction in which we should travel. We could hear the rustling and movement as the enemy went past, and a small dog belonging to Lieutenant Munro here nearly cost us our lives. Twice she gave little sharp growls, and I feared every moment she would begin to bark and so discover our hiding-place. I wanted to cut her throat, but Lieutenant Munro at length managed to gag her by covering her up in the breast of his coat. Slowly, very slowly as it seemed, night fell, and as the sun went down we could hear the wild elephants trumpeting as they came down from the hills to their feeding-grounds, and once the stillness was broken by the deep guttural roar of a tiger. It was hardly dark when we sallied forth from our hiding-place, and with some little difficulty at length regained the path. We had not gone very far when we found evidence that we were on the right road. Just about the place whence we had heard the two shots our baggage lay scattered right and left, as the coolies had thrown it away on the terror of their flight. Here was my bed, there lay my fiddle, in another place Munro's medicine chest was lying. I stayed here a short time to endeavour to find my diary and papers, but was unsuccessful. We were, however, lucky enough to find a small box of biscuits and a bottle of gin, and with this we pursued our way. As we proceeded the moon went down, and the jungle seemed to grow thicker and blacker; the elephant tracks also crossed each other in every direction, and we began to fear we had lost the path. Still we held on. Closer and closer grew the undergrowth, so that in some places one would have to wrestle with thick withy-like creepers that would wind round head and neck and arms, stopping all progress. Munro's hat, too, fell off, and it was so dark that we could not find it. On and on we toiled for hours and hours, until at last dead-beat we found we had a hill in front of us, and then were convinced that we were going in the wrong direction. We dropped down altogether, lying as close as we could for warmth's sake, and I soon fell into a heavy, dreamless sleep. The orderlies took in turn to watch. I was awakened about an hour before day-break by the dripping of the dew from the trees overhead; it pattered down almost like a smart shower wetting us through the cold, also was something fearful, and we had not eaten or drank since the morning before. However, a biscuit each and a dram of gin gave us some little strength, and we then took counsel as to our future proceedings. We could not go southward towards the boats as we knew the Shendoos had gone there before us in hot haste, not even stopping to plunder the baggage, while we knew that due west lay the Koladyne river. Westward then lay our course, though a mighty range of hills lay between us and the desired destination. However, we took heart and started. If our journey of the day before had been tedious our present route was doubly so; there was no path, and our road lay through a dense thicket of dead bamboos and up a hill slope of 45° or more. We had to creep sometimes on our bellies for ten minutes at a time, and sometimes had to cut a path with a sword which I had with me. We encouraged one another, however, to persevere, as there was but this hill between us and safety. We had been travelling about five hours up-hill the whole time and without a drop of water. The sun came down on us with a terrible heat, and poor Munro, being without his hat, suffered terribly. At length, however, we reached the top of the hill, and then to our utter dismay we discovered that before us lay another of equal dimensions. For aught we knew there might be another beyond that, and our strength was rapidly failing for want of food and drink. We sat down here, and cutting down a plantain tree we managed, by squeezing the stalk, to get a small quantity of moisture, and also we were fortunate enough to find some wild plantains nearly ripe, which we divided amongst us. From where we sat there was a most magnificent view of the whole valley of the Sulla Kheong, which we could see here and there like a silver thread winding its way up northward towards the Shendoo country, while beyond towered up range after range of mighty hills blue in the distance. As we looked out upon the prospect from the south came the sound of a heavy musketry fire. One conclusion we all arrived at, that Shendoos or no Shendoos, we must have water, for life was not worth keeping under the burning thirst from which we suffered. Munro put a bullet into his mouth, but that did not bring him any relief. Moreover, on account of my wound I could not climb any further, although I could go over a great deal more of comparatively level ground. We determined then to go down. We roused a tiger on our way, and he fortunately was as scared as we were, for had we been compelled to fire at him we should very quickly have had the Shendoos on us. We had got about two-thirds of the way down, when looking down through the trees we were startled to see three natives; one of them sat in the fork of a tree with his gun over his knee, while the two others stood beneath. At the same time from the jungle to the southward came the sound of many voices, so we turned and began painfully to ascend the hill again; but in a little while our strength failed us, and creeping into the jungle we lay down to wait the event. Soon, however, the sound of voices increased (there must have been a great many of them), came nearer, and then passed away towards the north. This was cheering, as we inferred that our enemies were on their way back. Towards night-fall, therefore, we descended with greater confidence, and after some little time we reached a stream of water, from which we did not think of moving for at least an hour. We could find no path, and so were compelled to guess at the direction in which we should go.

"There were no stars or moon, for a thick fog came over everything and bewildered us. Still we pushed on, the ground seemed to fall lower and lower, while the trees grew larger and the jungle thicker and more dark. We toiled away far into the night, until at last, feeling utterly lost and confused, we halted and lay down for the night. By great good luck I found four matches in my pocket, and as we were perishing with cold, and the jungle very dense, we determined to light a fire to warm ourselves and scare away wild beasts which we could hear moving in the jungle. Our biscuits were nearly finished, there being only three left, and we had no idea how long we might wander in this forest before reaching the Koladyne; so we determined the next day, if still unsuccessful, that we would kill Munro's little dog and cut her, and so gain some little strength for our struggle.

"We were all now much dispirited, and some of the natives who were with us began to give vent to expressions of despondency. We passed that night in the same manner as the previous one, the fire soon went out, as owing to our being in very low land we could get no dry wood. The cold was something terrible. When we awoke in the morning, and the jungle looked even more black and hopeless than it had done the night before, we started off, determining to follow downwards the first small stream we should cross until we should arrive at the Sulla Kheong, by following which we should eventually reach the Koladyne. So we followed a small nullah, and after a considerable time we came up a track or path beaten by many feet and leading due south. Into this we turned and had not gone far when we came upon one of the Mughs, who had been with us lying prone in the path. He had been knocked down with fever, and this, combined with three days' fasting, brought him into a somewhat exhausted condition. He was not of this part of the country, having followed the train of Munro in some menial capacity. He told us that when he could run no further, he had crawled into the jungle and hidden himself. He had hardly done so when about 200 Shendoos armed with muskets and spears had passed rapidly by on the same path which he had just left. He said that on the next day they returned accompanied by a great many more men, about 500 in all, bearing packages and goods, evidently our baggage. They must have divided in the pursuit, which would account for our being out-flanked. We did what we could for the new addition to our party, taking it by turns to lug him along. Fortunately we found in the path two or three handfuls of rice which had been spilled on the ground, and this was food for all of us. We had to proceed very cautiously, for although we knew now that we were in the right road (so large a body of men had made a well beaten track) we could not be sure that there was no outlying body of the enemy waiting to cut up stragglers; so two of us kept ahead as scouts, while the remainder painfully dragged themselves along behind. At length, however, we reached the Sulla Kheong at the place where we had left the boats about 1 p.m., but to our dismay not a boat was to be seen. On going a little way down stream we were fortunate enough to see one of our boats stranded on the opposite side, and this was soon brought over by one of the orderlies, who swam over for it. We found the paddles in the bottom of the canoe, and were soon on our way down stream as fast as we could go. A little further on we found all the boats scattered hither and thither as they had drifted down. The worst was now over, and then came the reaction. My leg literally was useless as a log of wood, perfectly numbed and without strength, and in hauling the canoe through the shallows into the big river Koladyne, I could give little or no assistance.

"That same evening we got down once more to Teynwey's village. The old man had returned and told us the following additional news:—That the major part of our fugitives, having lightened themselves of their loads, had safely reached the boats, but that as they were preparing to put off, the Shendoos arrived in hot haste and poured a volley upon them, when *sauve qui peut* was the order of the day, and every one fled into the jungle. He could not say what had become of all of them, but some had gone by his village on their way to their homes. After this we returned to Akyab with as much dispatch as possible, and I returned to Chittagong by the first steamer that offered, arriving there on the 11th of February, 1866. I had thus been absent a period of two months and twenty-seven days."

CONCLUSION.

Thus, with regret, I draw towards the close of my account of the Chittagong Hill Tribes. There is much that is loveable about them. They are very simple, and honest, and merry; but they have no sympathy with anything above the level of their bodily wants. There are whole tracts of mind, and thought, and feeling, which are unknown to them, and which could not be made known by any explanation. The idea that they are well enough as they are is a seductive one—to live according to Nature as the old Stoic philosophers taught; and if this idea could be perfected, if these people could be taught to live according to Nature in its higher sense, to rise above all gross and base indulgences, mindful of those higher laws of which only self-denial and self-command can render observance possible, I am not prepared to say but that this would be the wisest and the grandest ideal. We see in all other parts of the world that the introduction of civilization by means of European energy brings in its train a crowd of evils both mental and physical; yet everywhere throughout the world we force upon all the non-progressive races our intercourse, and finally our laws, with one grand object—Civilization. The latest authority on the subject, Sir Samuel Baker, says, "The primary object of geographical exploration is the opening to general intercourse such portions of the earth as may become serviceable to the human race. The explorer is the precursor of the colonist; the colonist is the human instrument by which the great work must be constructed, that greatest and most difficult of human undertakings, the civilization of the world." (Discovery of the Albert Nyanza, Introduction.) But what does civilization bring with it? Mr. Laing, in summing up the advantages of civilization in his "Theory of Business," after noting the increase of national wealth and the different scientific discoveries which have ministered thereto, adds, "True, there is now, as ever, a large class on the verge of starvation, but this is not incompatible with a state of great prosperity." I can imagine a hill man saying, "From such prosperity the Lord deliver me!" The motive power of civilization is the desire for wealth,—wealth, not as the necessaries, but for the delicacies and luxuries of life. "Le superflu, chose très necessaire," as Voltaire said. Among a simple people like our hill men there is no such desire; their nomadic life precludes any great accumulation of wealth, and they enjoy a perfect social equality. There is certainly no starvation among them; they occupy the "juste milieu" of neither poverty nor riches. Civilization brought into contact with these simple aboriginal races would not improve but exterminate them. In defining the object of exploration as "to discover and render serviceable to the human race unknown parts of the earth's surface," Sir Samuel Baker forgot to add that by the human race he implied only the civilized portion thereof. The question seems to me to be, what is the use of this God's earth? Is it not the happiness of the beings dwelling thereon? I doubt if civilization would render our hill men happier; not that I for a moment advocate leaving them undisturbed and unassisted in their present happy barbarism. Strength of mind is better than strength of body. But if one contrasts the simplicity and freedom of wild life with the hollow enjoyments and artificial joys of civilization ("Tædet me harum quotidianarum formarum"), it should not be forgotten that civilization has joys that are not artificial, and enjoyments that are not hollow. The pleasures of art, the enjoyments of nature, the subtler delights of the affections,—all these are unknown to the simple denizen of the hills, even to the last. In marriage with us, a perfect world springs up at the word, of tenderness, of fellowship, trust, and self-devotion. With them it is a mere animal and convenient connexion for procreating their species and getting their dinner cooked. They have no idea of tenderness, nor of the chivalrous devotion that prompted the old Galilean fisherman when he said, "Giving honour unto the woman as to the weaker vessel." It is the rule of the strongest that commands their reverence. Women are non-combatants; therefore contempt for them and their weakness marks all savages. The best of them will refuse to carry a burden if there be a wife, mother, or sister near at hand to perform the task. All this requires refinement and change; but, on the other hand, the position of women among them is preferable, in my opinion, to that occupied by the females of Hindoostan. Here is no mock modesty, but nature, pure and simple; the custom of concealing their women and hiding their faces, conveying as it does how much mistrust of man to man, exists only among the more effeminate races of Asia. Here, if a woman is condemned for her physical weakness, and forced, moreover, to bear the heaviest share of the toil for bread, she is still honoured as a wife and mother, trusted in her in-comings and out-goings, and her words of advice listened to with respect.

The relations that should exist between the sexes is one of the most important problems of the day, and it is therefore interesting to note the, to us, somewhat strange customs prevailing among these tribes. The reader will doubtless have found much to astonish, and perhaps somewhat to revolt, him in the strange moral and social habitudes of these races; but as in Noah's ark, where both the clean and the unclean beasts alike entered in, so we, to attain a true and faithful portraiture of these people, must take the bad with the good, their *mores*, manners or morals—their *virtus*, courage or virtue, together with the immorality, licence and intemperance, which form integral portions of all human natures, civilized or not. Ubi homines sunt, modi sunt. In one point notably these hill men are in consonance with us, in contradistinction to the custom generally observed by the nations of the East. I mean in the freedom of action, respectability of position, and consideration enjoyed by their womankind. If we turn our eyes to the nations of Hindoostan Proper, Persia, and Turkey, we shall find women reduced to the position of coveted chattels preserved for the convenience of the male sex. Here amongst these hill races, women enjoy almost perfect freedom of action; they go unveiled, they would seem to have equal rights of heritage with men, while their power of selecting their own husband is to the full as free as that enjoyed by our own English maidens. In Plutarch, the judge and panegyrist of so many illustrious men, we read that Gerudas, a primitive Spartan, on being asked by a stranger what punishment their law had for an adulterer, replied that it would be just as possible to find one in Sparta as to meet with a bull whose neck should be so long as to reach over the mountain Taygetas and drink from the river Eurotas, which lay on the other side of the mountain. So in these hills the crime of infidelity amongst wives is almost unknown; so also harlots and courtezans are held in abhorrence among them, and rendered unnecessary moreover by the freedom of intercourse indulged in and allowed to both sexes before marriage. These things are doubtless strange to us; their very dress, or perhaps I should say undress, might almost be called indecent; but it is not really so. Habit and temperature make usual and proper among them what we should consider the reverse. We cannot then condemn them on the score of indecency, for to the pure all things are pure. Our present notions of sexual decorum are highly artificial. The question of more or less clothes is one purely of custom and climate. If it were the custom for the legs of horses and dogs to be clothed, it would assuredly in a short time be stigmatized as gross indecency were they to appear in the streets without trousers. We, in England, wear many articles of clothing, simply because life could not be preserved in that climate without them; but here any large amount of clothing is absolutely insupportable. True modesty lies in the entire absence of thought upon the subject. Among medical students and artists the nude causes no extraordinary emotion; indeed it was a remark of Flaxman's, that the students in entering the academy seemed to hang up their passions along with their hats.

In considering the customs of a nation less advanced than ourselves, we are too apt to forget the time when the English word "wife" was derived from the Anglo-Saxon "wifian," to weave. We cannot forget that we are one of the dominant races of the world, and we look down consequently upon the subject races with an exclusive and haughty superciliousness as outer barbarians. A tithe of the care and beneficence expended upon the Hindoo would make of these hill races a noble and enlightened people. They have until lately been totally neglected, and yet a word of kindness, one sympathizing expression, and their hearts are open to you. My great and distinctive feeling with them has been that they were my fellow-creatures, men and women like myself: with the Bengallee I have never been in accord.

As far as I am able to judge, the civilizing instincts of the English have acted upon the unbreeched races with whom we have come in contact as conquerors, in two ways. By one method, as Sir Samuel Baker observes, "The explorer is the precursor of the colonist, and the colonist is the human instrument by which . . . ." right or wrong, whole races of men are driven from the lands of their ancestors. It is the old story of the earthen pot and the brazen vessel: contact with us is fatal to them; they are crushed down as with a hand of iron by laws and customs, to them alien and incomprehensible. Thus in America and New Zealand. Of the other method we have one grand example, which in its enormous inclusiveness is sufficient, viz., India. Here we have the strange spectacle of a great nation wishful to do good to the people subject to its rule, but powerless when the interests of trade are supposed to be endangered. India is a monument of English greatness and philanthropy, but it is also the outlet for the piece goods of Manchester, and the receptacle for Birmingham hardware. It is due to Englishmen to say that they do try to do good to the country and the people; but when it is a question of the people's benefit or an increased or diminished sale of Manchester cottons, piff! paff! the people are nowhere.

This I say, then, let us not govern these hills for ourselves, but administer the country for the well-being and happiness of the people dwelling therein. Civilization is the result and not the cause of civilization. What is wanted here is not measures but a man. Place over them an officer gifted with the power of rule; not a mere cog in the great wheel of Government, but one tolerant of the failings of his fellow-creatures, and yet prompt to see and recognize in them the touch of Nature that makes the whole world kin;—apt to enter into new trains of thought and to modify and adopt ideas, but cautious in offending national prejudice. Under a guidance like this, let the people by slow degrees civilize themselves. With education open to them, and yet moving under their own laws and customs, they will turn out, not debased and miniature epitomes of Englishmen, but a new and noble type of God's creatures.